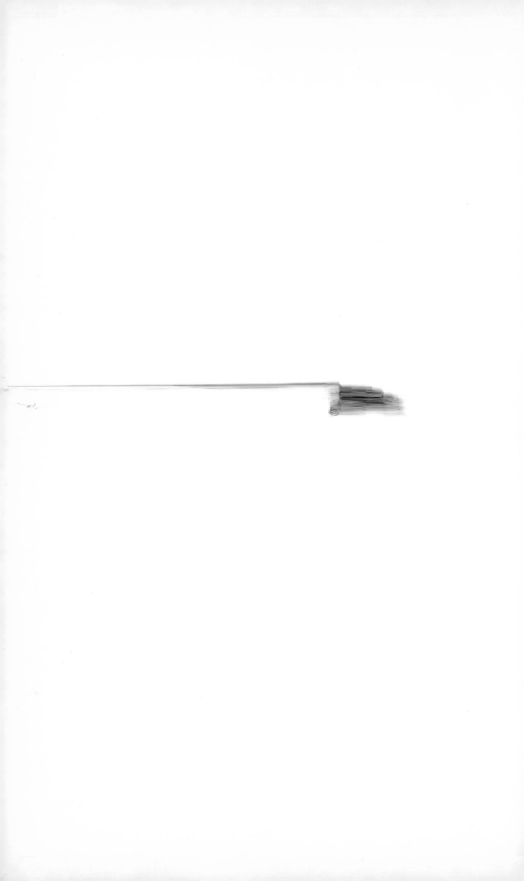

Management of Shipboard Maintenance

Management of Shipboard Maintenance

B.E.M.Thomas, B.Sc., M.Phil.,
Senior Lecturer, Department of
Maritime Studies, Liverpool Polytechnic.

STANFORD MARITIME LONDON

Stanford Maritime Limited
Member Company of the George Philip Group
12-14 Long Acre London WC2E 9LP
Editor D Nicolson

First Published 1980
© B.E.M.Thomas 1980
Filmset by Scribe Design, Gillingham, Kent
Printed in Great Britain by
Ebenezer Baylis and Son Ltd.,
The Trinity Press, Worcester & London

British Library Cataloguing in Publication Data

Thomas, B E M
    Management of shipboard maintenance.
    1. Ships — Maintenance and repair — Management
    I. Title
    658.2'02   VM299

ISBN 0–540–07354–7

Preface

Prior to writing this book the author carried out extensive research into the management of maintenance aboard merchant ships. He has studied the work and the points of view of the ship operator (at all levels), the manufacturer, the consultant and, perhaps most important, the shipboard personnel. One of the main conclusions arising from this research is that there is a very serious need for more and better training into the 'how' and, equally important, the 'why?' of maintenance management.

This book is intended to help to fulfil such a need. It is aimed primarily at the seafarer, since it is upon him that the final onus rests, and also at shore-based superintendents as well as other ship-operator personnel, who help to devise and run ship maintenance management systems.

It is felt that the management of spares should be an integral part of maintenance management and is therefore also considered.

Many shipping companies have installed planned maintenance and spares control systems on their ships, some covering just the engine room and some the entire ship, including paintwork and electronic equipment. The levels of sophistication and complexity of these maintenance and spares systems vary enormously. The levels of effectiveness and acceptance by sea staff also vary widely, often without any obvious connection. It is hoped that this book will help those involved to understand the philosophies behind their companies' maintenance policies and to make the most of those policies, whether they involve comprehensive planned maintenance and spares control systems or, at the other end of the scale, no formal systems at all but maintenance left to the chief engineers' or mates' discretion.

The art of maintenance management cannot be learned purely by experience, and simple common sense alone does not always provide the correct solution to maintenance problems. Add to this the fact that merchant ships are extremely valuable to their owners, both in initial cost and earning capability, and need to have a high level of reliability, often isolated from shore-based maintenance and spares facilities. Thus it can be seen that training is vital. All those involved in shipboard maintenance must be able not only to perform their roles in the best way, but also to understand why they are doing it and their importance with regard to the success of the maintenance operation as a whole (particularly in formal planned maintenance systems). It is sincerely hoped that this book will enable those who read it to subsequently improve their performance and understanding of the management of ship maintenance.

Liverpool 1980   B.E.M. THOMAS

Acknowledgements

The author extends his sincerest thanks to:

Sir Joseph W. Isherwood (International) Ltd.,
B.P. Tanker Company Ltd.,
Marine Audio Visual Instructional Systems Ltd.,
Blue Star Ship Management Ltd.,
The Marconi International Marine Company Ltd.,
S.S. Stevenson & Partners Ltd.,
Houlders Brothers & Co. Ltd.,
Kardex Systems (U.K.) Ltd. and
the Merchant Navy Training Board for their
unstinted co-operation and help.

He also wishes to thank all the members of the
Maritime Studies Department of Liverpool Poly
technic who gave their assistance and, in particular,
Mr. B. Tabernacle of the Management Studies
Department, for his invaluable advice.

Contents

1 The Importance of Effective Maintenance Management 1
2 Planned Maintenance   18
3 Spares Control   38
4 System Types   49
5 Relevant Management Principles   99
6 Shipboard Management   119
7 Requirements of Regulatory Bodies   126
8 Conclusions for the Future   135
   Bibliography   141
   Index   142

Chapter 1
The Importance of Effective
Maintenance Management

1.1 *The Need*

Almost every plant or unit in industry requires maintenance of some description. There are basically two types of industry, the *production* industry and the *service* industry. The overall functions of equipment must be ultimately to output a product, be it a jumbo jet or a ball bearing. In the service industry the equipment provides, or helps to provide, a service. Both industries endeavour to supply their product or service at an 'optimum cost' (i.e. a competitive cost enabling them to achieve their short and long term objectives) but apart from this their aims differ. Whereas the production industry is concerned with the efficiency of manufacturing operations, the service industry is concerned with the efficiency of the service it provides (see Figure 1).

Shipping is a transport industry and transport is a service industry, therefore the ultimate aims of shipping must be to

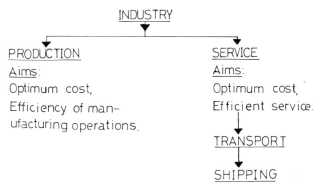

Fig. 1: Industrial Aims

1

provide an efficient service at an optimum cost. When considering maintenance, it is vital that these aims are borne in mind. Without any maintenance a ship would cease to function after a very short space of time, but unless the *right* maintenance policy is applied to that ship, she has very little chance of providing an efficient service at an optimum cost. Not only will costs directly connected with maintenance rise, but also the ship will be operating below her best, hence raising the cost of the service she is providing. (Direct, measurable, maintenance costs have been estimated to be around a quarter of the total operating costs.)

Shipping transport has several specific problems with regard to maintenance which make effective ship maintenance policies essential. These will be expanded later in this chapter but briefly they are:

(i) The high degree of isolation from repair and spares facilities.

(ii) The high cost of a transport unit (i.e. the ship).

(iii) The heavy cost of a ship out of service.

(iv) Varying costs and quality of labour and spares throughout the world.

(v) Shipboard personnel are operators as well as maintainers.

(vi) The frequency with which personnel join and leave ships, creating a need for continuity of ships' maintenance plans.

(vii) Severe safety and insurance conditions, necessitating rigorous survey requirements.

These problems obviously vary for different ships and routes. A shipping company must therefore adopt a maintenance policy for each ship, considering all the objectives and problems, always bearing in mind the ultimate aims of *efficiency at an optimum cost.*

1.2 *The Objectives*

The objectives of any effective maintenance policy may be broadly stated as follows:

(i) To ensure the availability of equipment.

(ii) To ensure an adequate level of equipment efficiency.

(iii) To control the rate of equipment deterioration.

(iv) To combine the above objectives so that an optimum cost may be achieved.

The first three objectives, if achieved, fulfil our first aim of providing an efficient service. The last objective implies a successful balance of the first three so that, while still providing an efficient service, the cost is optimised, our second aim. Let us now look at each objective more closely.

Consideration of equipment availability brings us to *downtime*, a term much used by maintenance managers and engineers. The British Standards define this as *the period during which a facility is not ready for use*, i.e. the period of time a piece of equipment is unusable while it receives or awaits maintenance of some description. Downtime of *all* machinery need not necessarily be minimised. Usually we attempt to minimise the downtime of essential equipment, since if this is not functioning, the system of which it forms a part ceases to operate. However, downtime of non-essential equipment must be brought to the most economical level, considering availability of spares, manpower, etc.

The required level of equipment efficiency should also be carefully considered. In most cases maintenance raises the level of efficiency, but the more maintenance that is carried out, the more maintenance costs and downtime will probably arise. Also, increasing the efficiency of a piece of equipment past a certain point has very little effect on the efficiency of the whole system or operation. Take, for example, the cleaning and painting of a ship's underwater form. This is an expensive operation and can consume valuable downtime of the ship. If it is not carried out frequently enough the service speed of the ship would fall to an uneconomic level, but if carried out too frequently only a small increase in service speed would result which would not justify the expense.

The rate of equipment deterioration must be controlled to lie within the best economic limits. In most cases, the absence of maintenance would result in excessive deterioration, while

3

too much maintenance might simply be wasting money. To keep in perfect condition a piece of equipment which, after a limited time, will be written off and replaced with a newer design, is uneconomic. Sometimes, over-maintenance of inherently poor equipment could be looked upon as throwing good money after bad. Thus the allowable rate of equipment deterioration often depends on such things as capital expenditure and the rate of equipment design development.

It can be seen from the above that the first three objectives are inter-related and all directly related to the fourth objective of achieving optimum cost. A balance of these objectives must be reached or, as it were, the correct 'mix' achieved. When considering what this balance or mix should be it is important that the maintenance operation should not be looked at in isolation, but rather in the light of all the ship's other operations and the whole service which the company provides. To take an obvious example, cargo work would generally be of higher priority than non-essential maintenance in port, and so on.

Maintenance, like any other operation, must be managed effectively, both from the economic standpoint and from the point of view that if it is not then chaos will ultimately reign. The advantages of effective maintenance management, implied in the objectives, are clearly the most important but there are many more that automatically follow, often on a more personal level, such as increased job satisfaction and more even work loads. These will be discussed later.

1.3 *Basic Maintenance Policies*

To discover how the objectives discussed in the previous section can be achieved, we must first consider the different basic maintenance policies which it is possible to adopt (see Figure 2).

We are faced with two sets of alternatives. Firstly, we may either replace the item being considered or we may maintain the one we already have. Both are essentially maintenance policies. To refer again to British Standards, maintenance is defined as *work undertaken in order to keep or restore every facility to an acceptable standard.* This could involve replacements of parts of that facility as well as overhauling and repairing (i.e. maintenance as opposed to replacement) of existing parts.

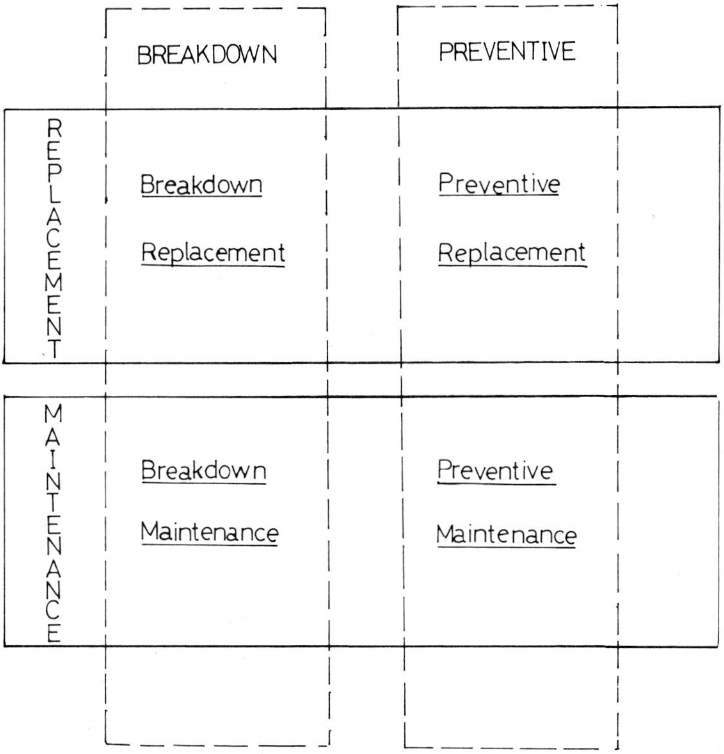

Fig. 2: Basic Maintenance Policies

It is perhaps interesting to consider that replacement is invariably applied at both extremes. Considering a ship for example, ultimately she must be replaced since she cannot be maintained for ever, indeed the owner would not want her to be as she would eventually be outdated. At the other extreme, when we split that ship into components, sub-components and so on, we will come eventually to items which can only be replaced if they fail, e.g. 'O' rings, liners and bearings. In between, we may choose either a replacement or a maintenance policy. Of course, if we adopt a maintenance policy

5

for, say, a winch this does not necessarily mean that no components of that winch will be replaced. They almost certainly will. It simply means that we have opted to maintain the winch rather than replace the whole thing periodically or when it fails.

The second set of alternatives concerns *when* we replace or maintain. Do we do it when a failure occurs, i.e. adopt a *breakdown* policy, or do we do it before a failure, thus preventing its occurrence, i.e. a *preventive* policy? It should be said, however, that sometimes it is impossible to predict when failure will occur, but we still have the choice of either accepting this fact and adopting a breakdown policy or deciding on what seems to be a reasonable period between preventive actions. From these alternatives we have a choice of four basic policies:

Breakdown Replacement. This policy could be adopted when a breakdown would not cause expensive repercussions, and when the cost of repairing equipment exceeds the cost of replacing it. This might apply to cheap, easily replaceable items. It could also apply to an item whose design is in a stage of rapid development, i.e. when it fails it is out of date anyway and should be replaced with a newer design.

Preventive Replacement. This implies replacing equipment before breakdowns are expected. It could be suitable for equipment which operates as an independent unit. Perhaps the easiest example to take is a motor car, one of a commercial fleet or a private vehicle, where a breakdown is expensive, inconvenient and costly. Coupled with this is the fact that after a certain amount of wear, the rate of failures occurring could very well accelerate and the car devalue considerably. Another example is sealed units or units which are difficult to maintain or repair and which form a vital part in a particular operation. A common problem with this policy is to know how often to replace. How often have we heard motorists debating the best time to change their cars? With more complex equipment there is usually no simple answer, as the future reliability cannot be accurately assessed with certainty. With

6

relatively simple sealed units etc., an expected life span can often be assessed (bearing in mind that there are always exceptions—electronic equipment can have a devastatingly random life span) and the replacement period would be planned within this life span.

Both breakdown replacement and preventive replacement give the benefits of having modern equipment and low maintenance costs (basic servicing, lubrication, etc., would be carried out on most items).

Breakdown Maintenance. If a replacement policy is not suitable then the alternative must be to maintain the present equipment. A breakdown maintenance policy would be suitable for equipment which, should it break down, would not stop, or adversely affect to a large extent, any important operation to which it contributed. Safety is also a factor. If a breakdown would cause a safety hazard, this policy would not be appropriate. Bearing this in mind, breakdown maintenance is basically suitable when all the costs involved in a breakdown occurring, and rectifying it, are less than the cost of endeavouring to avoid a breakdown (see 'Preventive maintenance'). It could be adopted where equipment is 'doubled up' (i.e. when one fails, the other is brought into use while the first one is being repaired), or where a rapid spares facility is available so that downtime would be very short when a breakdown occurred.

The word 'breakdown' here should be taken to include a situation where the efficiency of the equipment falls to an intolerable level or a level below, for example, a legal safety requirement. Basic servicing would normally be carried out on most items within this policy.

Preventive Maintenance. When the failure of a piece of equipment could prove very expensive or when a failure would cause a safety hazard, this policy would normally be applied (assuming preventive replacement was not appropriate). It is the maintenance alternative to breakdown maintenance. If the equipment being considered was essential to an important operation or system, a breakdown of this equipment would incur extremely high downtime costs, since the operation or system would be unworkable until the equipment was repaired. Under these conditions a preventive maintenance policy would be most suitable. Simply, if the cost of a breakdown and its rectification is more than the cost of endeavouring to prevent it, preventive maintenance is preferable to breakdown maintenance.

What this policy involves is anticipating breakdowns and attempting to avoid them by inspection, servicing and overhaul, i.e. keeping the equipment in such a condition that breakdown should not be reasonably expected to occur.

1.4 *Preventive Maintenance.*

It is felt necessary to elaborate on preventive maintenance since this is the most common policy adopted in ships. As already stated the aim is to avoid breakdowns occurring by inspection, servicing, overhaul and, possibly, by replacement of some components (of the unit considered). Depending on the depth and type of maintenance being carried out this may or may not involve downtime, i.e. it may either be *running* or *shut-down* maintenance. If shut-down maintenance is necessary then one should try to minimise downtime costs by arranging the maintenance when the unit is not in use or when it is non-essential; e.g. the obvious time to carry out preventive maintenance of the main engine is when the ship is in port, whereas preventive maintenance of cargo gear would best be done at sea. If this is not possible then plainly it should be carried out as quickly as possible.

Perhaps the major problem with preventive maintenance (and indeed often with preventive replacement, as mentioned earlier) is anticipating failure and thus deciding when the maintenance should be done. There are essentially two techniques which can be applied (see Figure 3), *scheduling*, i.e. carrying out the maintenance at regular intervals, or *monitoring* the equipment and carrying out maintenance when it reaches a certain level.

Scheduling may be based on calendar time (e.g. every 3 months) or running time (e.g. every 2,000 running hours or, as

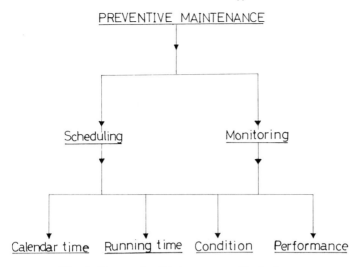

Fig. 3: Preventive Maintenances Techniques

in a car, every 3,000 miles). Running time is more difficult to achieve for several reasons. Firstly, it can be difficult to estimate unless a meter, a log, or something of this kind is used. Secondly, it is more difficult to plan (see Chapter 2 - Planned Maintenance). Thirdly, there is a temptation for the maintenance manager in direct control of the work (e.g. the Chief Engineer) to convert the running time into calendar time so that he may plan the work more easily. This temptation should be resisted unless the conversion can be done accurately - in which case it should not have been in running time in the first place! Calendar time is often more suitable for long term planning but its main disadvantage is that it does not allow for spasmodic usage of equipment, whereas running time does.

The big question with scheduling is how to know the maintenance tasks and their corresponding frequencies. Or to put it another way, 'What needs to be done and how often?' The answer usually comes from several different sources, none of which should be ignored; they are:

(i) *The manufacturers* - their advice and particularly their warranty conditions.

9

(ii) *The insurers* - scheduling is often built around classification society surveys which must be complied with to remain insured.

(iii) *The government(s) concerned* - governmental surveys should be included in the schedule.

(iv) *Experience* - last but certainly not least this is a vital ingredient and often may be more reliable than the manufacturers' advice, particularly if his equipment is not 'marinised', or designed specifically for use at sea.

Often experience must be drawn upon at the end of the day, since manufacturers' advice can vary from an 'overkill' to a vague 'thumbnail sketch'.

The monitoring of equipment, as an alternative method of deciding when and what maintenance is necessary may be very simple or involve the use of quite sophisticated monitoring equipment. It can, however, be split into two categories; *condition monitoring* and *performance monitoring*. Condition monitoring means keeping a continuous or periodic watch on the equipment's condition. When that equipment, or part of it, reaches a predetermined state, the necessary maintenance is carried out to bring it back to 'scratch' or 'A1' condition. It may involve installing vibrational analysis equipment or just looking and listening. Most people at some time or another have listened to an unusual knocking in some piece of machinery and said to themselves, 'Time I did something about that'. One could even go so far as to say that this could be described as 'vibrational analysis in the audio range'!

It should be mentioned here that condition monitoring, which is an 'on-going' process, should not be confused with condition analysis which is, if you like, a 'one shot' operation of analysing the deterioration (particularly the rate of deterioration and the point at which failure occurs) so that the maintenance frequencies for scheduling can be established. It is really a technique of gaining experience of the equipment rapidly and in detail.

Performance monitoring differs from condition monitoring in that here we are looking at the output or efficiency of the equipment rather than its state. Let us take, as an example, our earlier case of the cleaning of a ship's underwater form. If we were deciding when to clean and re-apply antifouling we could either say that we will do it when we discover, by sending a diver down, a certain amount of fouling (i.e. condition monitoring), or that we will do it when the service speed drops below a certain figure (i.e. performance monitoring). Again, performance monitoring techniques may be sophisticated, involving torque gauges for instance, or very basic such as simply asking oneself 'does it do what I want it to', although in this latter case we are approaching a 'breakdown policy'. In general, using performance monitoring techniques it is not possible to pinpoint where maintenance is necessary, since only the output is being monitored, whereas using condition monitoring we can, very often, achieve this.

No matter whether condition or performance monitoring is adopted, the level of state or output at which to apply maintenance still has to be decided. This, again, usually comes from experience, although sometimes manufacturers may give guidance. The most common way is to monitor until failure occurs and then attempt to estimate a 'safe' level just before the failure level.

A major advantage of monitoring is that maintenance is only carried out when needed. This means that it can cope with spasmodic usage and usage of varying severity. However, like running time, it can be difficult to plan. Also, one is limited, by the type of machinery being considered, as to what type of monitoring is possible.

A certain amount of scheduled maintenance very often has to be combined with maintenance by monitoring techniques since the warranty, insurance and legal requirements still must be met, and these usually involve periodic maintenance and surveys.

1.5   *The Factors*

We have already discussed the objectives of maintenance management and the basic policy options it is possible to adopt. We started off (in 1.1) by looking at shipping's special maintenance problems, thus establishing the very definite need for having effective ship maintenance policies. So, assuming that this is what a shipping company should be aiming at, how must they set about the task? First they must realise that the right policy for them must be tailor-made, i.e. it must fit the factors influencing their ships, or possibly be different for individual ships. A book could be written solely on the factors influencing ships' maintenance policies, since there are many and they each vary in importance for each type of company, ship, run, etc., but to be brief they are as follows. (Note that these embody some of the problems discussed in 1.1)

Degree of Isolation. Ships, because of their very nature, are isolated in several respects. They are often isolated from repair and maintenance facilities ashore, in many cases not only while at sea but also in many of the remoter ports. Isolation from such facilities depends mainly on the type of operation and run a vessel is engaged on. Ships are also isolated from extensive spares facilities. The extent of this isolation again depends on the operation and run, and also on such things as whether a shipping company has spares 'dumps' around the world, as some do. Finally, ships may be isolated with regard to communication, from their head office, manufacturers etc. Even in these modern days of telex, wireless telephone and so on, effective advice and help with a maintenance problem is still often far away.

To show, generally, how the degree of isolation may vary from one type of ship and her operation to another, compare a Continent/U.K. ferry with a tramp plying the Borneo coast. The comparison speaks for itself.

It is largely the degree of isolation that determines the extent to which shipboard maintenance features in the overall maintenance policy, i.e. how much maintenance must be carried out by, or under the control of, the shipboard personnel.

Ship Costs. The cost of a ship and much of her equipment is extremely high, representing a considerable investment on

12

the part of her owner and this investment must be protected. A failure of a vital piece of equipment could put the whole ship at risk. Consider a main engine failure in a busy channel or a radar failure in fog. Of course, the risks cannot be eliminated, and emergency equipment and procedures should be used wherever possible, but it is prudent to minimise them by optimising reliability. Ship costs vary enormously, specialised vessels costing a phenomenal amount, and it is worth noting that such vessels are very often the ones with the greatest risks and therefore require the highest degree of reliability. Take, for example, an ice-breaker or a liquid gas carrier. Both these vessels would have a very high replacement cost, not to mention other costly repercussions that might follow the disaster resulting from a major failure.

Cost of Downtime. This again is generally very high for a vessel but varies with the type of operation and where it occurs. Downtime in port is usually more costly than that at sea (although it can be shorter if maintenance facilities are available) but whenever a ship is not fulfilling her intended role, i.e. not earning, then she is costing the company money. Downtime costs are also relative to the size of the company and her operation. A small cross-channel car ferry company owning, say, four vessels would be very badly hit financially if one of their ships was inoperable for a month at the height of the holiday season. A month's downtime of an oil tanker belonging to the fleet of a large international oil company, while by no means desirable, would be but a small hiccup compared to the fate of the ferry company.

Shore Labour and Spares Costs. These costs vary around the world. In some cases it is possible to pay more for shore labour in one port, than in another where the labour and maintenance facilities are better. With regard to spares, one is very often paying for transportation costs, which can increase the total cost considerably. Some machinery parts are made under license in different parts of the world, however experience sometimes shows that these are not as good as the original manufacturer's own spares. As was mentioned briefly

13

in discussion of the degree of isolation, some companies store spares around the world, or belong to a spares supply network.

Since a company's shore labour and spares costs may vary, depending on the ports they use, they are, like the degree of isolation, an influencing factor when deciding how much of the maintenance should be carried out by sea staff and also the extent of spares carried aboard ship; i.e. the degree to which the maintenance policy should be biased towards shipboard activity.

'Flying squads' of maintenance workers, either contracted in or a shipping company's own men, are sometimes used and can be the most economical option where the regular crew are already fully stretched and local shore labour is expensive or inadequate.

Ships' Personnel. The crew of a ship differs from the 'crews' of most other types of transport unit in that they must not only be operators but, in the vast majority of cases, also maintainers. The extent of the maintenance which they perform varies with the other factors discussed here. Also, the shipowner must abide by legal minimum manning levels. If he were only to use the crew for watchkeeping they would not be fully employed, thus it is logical that they should also contribute to the maintenance of the ship to fully utilise their time. (This, incidentally, implies training of sea staff to be included in the maintenance policy, which will be covered later in the book).

The problem of the frequent changing of personnel aboard a ship must also be considered. The length of time a crew member stays aboard one ship varies with company policy and very often with that person's own wishes, but the maintenance policy chosen must, as well as simply providing the necessary continuity, be suited to the frequency of crew 'turn-over'; e.g. a policy giving a chief engineer an annual budget is not realistic if the chief engineer changes every three months.

Uniformity Of Ships. Varying types, ages, conditions, operations and routes, of ships within any one fleet, can create problems for the policy maker. As stated earlier, he may have to adopt different policies for different ships, but obviously problems of documentation and overall control of the fleet's maintenance are eased if one basic policy can be chosen for the whole fleet. This policy will have to be flexible enough to be easily modified and built upon so that it can be successfully applied to the fleet's range of vessels. The more uniform a company's ships, the more detailed and sophisticated the basic policy may become.

1.6   Developing a Policy

Having realised the factors (discussed in the previous section), the maintenance policy maker must then try to quantify them for his particular case, or put them into the correct perspective bearing in mind the ship or ships, route, operation, etc. Once he has achieved this, then what is required should start to become clearer. He must look at the problem at several different levels - the ship(s), the items of shipboard equipment and the components which form that equipment. He must then choose, at each level and for each case, a preventive or a breakdown policy and whether that policy should be based on maintenance or replacement. At ship level, he must decide on a spares policy and how much to bias his maintenance and spares policies towards shipboard activity.

The prospect of considering each item of equipment and each component perhaps sounds more daunting than it is, since in practice, of course, many items may be lumped together. Also, at basic component level only replacement is possible.

Let us take as an example a general cargo vessel trading mainly in a part of the world where maintenance facilities and skills are poor, but labour is cheap. Her company is of a moderate size. Her average length of voyage is six months, returning to a British port after each voyage. A probable policy in this case would be, firstly, one biased fairly heavily towards shipboard maintenance and with a reasonably comprehensive set of spares carried aboard. Since ship downtime costs would most likely be high for the company, all

15

essential equipment at least, should be covered by a preventive maintenance policy. This could also be extended to non-essential equipment whose repair costs are high. However, since unskilled shore labour is cheap this could be used for some maintenance work - possible painting or cleaning deep tanks - provided the ship's crew could be fully utilised on other work. We are, of course, simplifying here. A real life situation would be more complex, with many other factors to be considered, but this example does show how the policy maker's mind should be working.

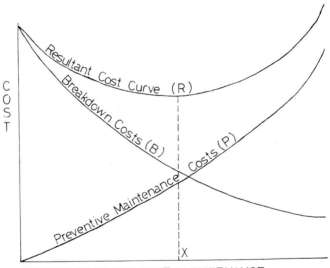

DEGREE OF PREVENTIVE MAINTENANCE

B= Repair costs + Spares costs + Loss of earnings
    due to downtime etc..

P= Maintenance costs + Spares costs + Loss of
    earnings due to downtime etc.

R= Resultant of B and P.

"X" marks optimum degree of preventive maintenance.

Fig. 4: Operational Research Example of Finding Optimum Level of Preventive Maintenance

16

A good maintenance policy will help to optimise the overall cost of the service being provided by the shipping company in the following ways:

(i) A reduction in maintenance costs.
(ii) A reduction in running costs.
(iii) A higher level of efficiency.
(iv) A smaller downtime.

It is important to realise that a balance of these is necessary. If one tries to maximise one, the others will almost certainly suffer as a result. This balance can only be fully achieved when all the factors are realised and quantified, and even then the solution is often still not obvious. Operational research methods may be used to good effect here.

Figure 4 shows a simple example of how a resultant costs and loss of earnings curve can be obtained. By finding the lowest point on this curve the optimum balance between preventive maintenance and breakdown maintenance can be established. The initial cost and loss of earnings curves could either be established from actual data (then possibly extending the curves), or by algebraic methods. In complex cases involving several variables, this method could easily be adapted for computer techniques.

Chapter 2
Planned Maintenance

2.1 *The Meaning*

Most seafarers have heard the term 'planned maintenance'. Many, unfortunately, respond to it with a groan. Perhaps this is because it is surrounded by misconceptions. Its correct definition (from British Standards again) is *'maintenance work organised and carried out with forethought, control and records'*. What a large number of seafarers understand it to mean is scheduled maintenance, invariably accompanied by an awesome amount of paperwork. Let us lay this myth to rest before proceeding further. Planned maintenance (p.m.) is any kind of maintenance policy, or any combination of basic policies (as described in Chapter 1), that is planned, controlled and recorded. It may be a very simple system, perhaps confined to an engineer's head and notebook, or a highly sophisticated one, with grandiose planning boards, record sheets, etc., installed by the company at great expense.

The basic aims of p.m. are the same as those of maintenance management. In other words, it is a tool to help with effective maintenance management; a tool which should be fashioned and used to meet a given set of maintenance criteria. It must be looked upon in this way, both by the designers of the system and the users of it. If it is, then it should succeed in its objectives. If it is not, it will most certainly fail.

To return to the definition. The main components of p.m. will be discussed later (in 2.3); let us look now at the basic ingredients: *forethought, control* and *records* (see Figure 5).

Forethought, or planning, is essential to any operation. We must look ahead. If we do not, but simply try to tackle
18

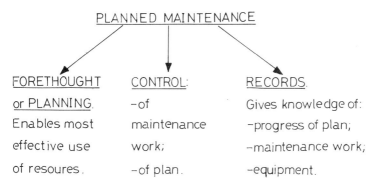

Fig. 5: Ingredients of Planned Maintenance

each problem as it comes along, we will not be prepared for it and hence cannot hope to do a good job. Even with a breakdown policy planning is necessary, since one must endeavour to ensure that the manpower, spares, facilities, etc. are available when the breakdown occurs. Planning maintenance enables us to use our resources most effectively.

Any system must both exert control, and itself be controlled. The whole purpose of maintenance management is to control the maintenance operation and, as already stated, a planned maintenance system should enable this to be done. However, it can only achieve this if it is itself controlled. It cannot, as it were, be 'put into automatic' and left to run. The system must be monitored and adjusted whenever and wherever necessary.

Recording is vital both to planning and control. It is said that a good politician is usually a good historian. This is because in order to know the best way in which to proceed one must know what has gone before. To be able to formulate and amend a plan one must have real knowledge as to the likelihood of success of different options. We are all wiser in hindsight, the trick is to use that wisdom! Equally important, to continue with a predetermined plan one must have up-to-date knowledge of how far the plan has progressed. By recording relevant details of maintenance tasks and equipment condition (provided we then use this data properly) we

19

are not only aware of how the plan is progressing but eventually have a maintenance history which can be analysed, revealing possible weaknesses in the plan or equipment. Thus we have the knowledge to amend the plan or, possibly, formulate a new one. Looked at in this way, it can be seen that recording facilitates control of the work, by providing information on how the work is progressing and – by analysis of past records – suggesting the best ways it can be done. It also facilitates control of the plan, by fulfilling the need for 'feedback' on how successfully it is achieving its objectives.

Planned maintenance is, therefore, simply maintenance management tackled in a logical and scientific manner, encompassing any of the basic maintenance policies.

2.2 *Benefits*

The main benefit of p.m. is, of course, that it enables maintenance management to be effective. However, in this section we will endeavour to itemise the most important individual advantages. Remember though that these are general p.m. benefits, and not those of p.m. using any particular policy, e.g. preventive p.m.

Increased Efficiency of Equipment. Assuming that the correct maintenance policies have been incorporated into the p.m. system, which is implied under 'forethought', increased efficiency of equipment should result.

Greater Availability of Equipment. Good planning should lead to maintenance being carried out when it is most convenient to do so, except for unpredictable breakdowns. Downtime should be reduced because spares, facilities and manpower can be planned, thus when maintenance work arises it can be carried out in the minimum time. Also, equipment included in a p.m. system should generally experience fewer unpredicted breakdowns. All this leads to reduced downtime costs.

Less Expensive Emergency Repairs. Unplanned emergency repairs will almost always prove expensive since the chances are that they will occur at the most inconvenient times, say when manpower is not available or is likely to incur overtime costs, when the necessary spares are not on board, and so on. In short, they usually comply with that well known seafaring law concerning a lump of turf! Under a p.m. system, the number of repairs of this type should be reduced.

Proper Coverage of Equipment. All equipment included in a p.m. system should receive adequate maintenance coverage, with no equipment being overlooked. This is not to say that each piece of equipment will have the same basic policy applied to it, but rather that it will have the most suitable policy applied to it, in the light of its contribution to the whole operation. The required differentials, so to speak, between different equipments' maintenance requirements, and their subsequent performance, reliability, etc., will be maintained.

Effective Use of Labour. If maintenance work is planned the work load can be evenly distributed, avoiding periods of high and low activity levels (see Figure 6). Constantly varying peaks and troughs of maintenance activity, as well as being unsound economically speaking, is also unsettling to the work force. Notice, in Figure 6, that the area under each curve represents the total man-hours over the period considered. In the majority of cases, the total man-hours with p.m. should be less than the total man-hours without p.m., i.e. the total work load is reduced by adopting p.m., since, among other reasons, the right number of men are available when required and are working within normal working hours, so the work can be completed more efficiently. (Supporters of general purpose crews would also argue that such crews give greater flexibility to work planning).

Also, the allocation of maintenance work may be carried out more effectively. In the long term, necessary skill levels and manning levels can be established. In the short term, a week or a day's work may be planned out, sending the most suitable men to tackle that work.

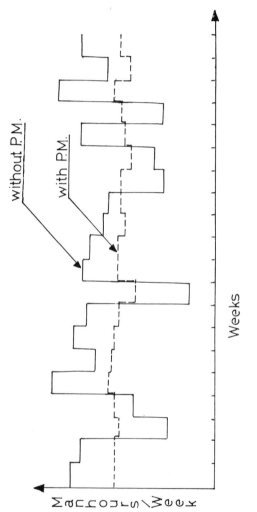

Fig. 6: Workloads With and Without PM

Continuity. The problem of personnel joining and leaving ships, creating a need for continuity of the ship's maintenance plans, has already been raised in Chapter 1; p.m. surmounts this problem since, provided that the records have been kept up to date, relieving personnel can see how far the plan has progressed and simply 'pick up the reins' where the relieved personnel have left off. This is made all the easier when similar p.m. systems are installed on all of a company's ships (similar documentation, planning boards, etc.) because relieving personnel should then already be familiar with the p.m. system that they are taking over.

Higher Morale. Good communications are vital to the success of a p.m. system. This aspect will be discussed at length later but, assuming a p.m. system does have effective communications and everybody involved is aware of how and why they should perform their functions within the system, their job satisfaction, commitment and general morale should be high. Also, as has already been mentioned, the more even work-load that p.m. gives has a favourable effect upon personnel's morale. In these modern times, we hear and read a lot about the adverse effects of 'stress'. Personal stress in a working situation is often brought on by disorder and a lack of control of one's problems; p.m. is intended to give order and control to the maintenance operation and, therefore, provided this is realised and the p.m. system used correctly, personal stress of the maintenance manager and worker can largely be removed. This can only have a favourable effect on his morale, which is true for both ship and shore personnel.

Planning of Spares. If the maintenance work is planned, then the majority of spares requirements are known in advance. It therefore becomes possible to order spares ahead of time, to carry aboard ship only the spares that are likely to be needed, and to carry them in the right numbers. In other words, without p.m. it is impossible to formulate an effective spares stock control system. As well as from the planning of future maintenance work, spares requirements can also be estimated from the p.m. records, assuming that those used for each job have been recorded. This is one benefit of the analysis of p.m. records. The following benefits are also attributable to such analysis.

Highlighting Weaknesses and High Cost Areas. Items that are not proving to be as reliable as expected, or need more maintenance than expected, may be highlighted by analysis of p.m. records. Usually, it should also be possible to pinpoint the component(s) where the trouble lies, and to decide whether it is the maintenance methods or policy that is at fault, or a weakness inherent in the equipment. High cost areas may be identified by, for example, reports indicating excessive concentration of maintenance on a particular item, or by actually costing the various maintenance functions, spares, etc. and carrying out a cost analysis. Thus it becomes possible to change or modify both the equipment and the plan in such a way as to minimise maintenance costs.

Information of this kind is extremely useful when ordering spares and when drawing up specifications for new vessels.

Budget Control. Budgeting is an important part of any management function, maintenance management not excluded, and this aspect will be discussed in depth later in the book. However, to allocate and plan a maintenance budget one requires knowledge of probable necessary expenditure. The maintenance plan and analysis of maintenance records yield this information. More immediate analysis of recent records also facilitates monitoring, and hence control, of the budget.

Forecasting Ability. We have already stated that analysis of records helps us to formulate future plans. What we are very often doing is extracting a forecast from the analysis and planning on the basis of the forecast. Analysis of the past is invariably the best if not the only way of forecasting the future, but one should bear in mind, however, that what can be extracted from the records is totally dependent upon what has been put in, and the accuracy of any forecast drawn from an analysis of records depends upon what has been recorded and how.

2.3   The Basic Components

It is very difficult to break p.m. down into discrete components, as these vary considerably, often fulfilling more than one function within the system. It should therefore be borne in mind, when reading the following sections, that a component of an actual system may not be indentical to a component described here; but it might, for example, be a combination of two.

The approach taken here is to look first at the initial documentary components that it is necessary to compile at the development stage of a p.m. system, and then at the essential components of a fairly comprehensive shipboard p.m. system in operation, each component fulfilling a particular function (see Figure 7). The development stage, then, consists of the compilation of the following.

Register of Equipment to be Included. Before such a register can be compiled, a complete inventory of all equipment must be taken, so that one may start off with a complete picture. A lot of relevant information may be had from existing records, but often an actual survey or physical check on equipment has to be carried out. Sometimes on-site photographs can assist this process. Each item must be identified and described. Identification can be aided by introducing a coding system, but a word of warning here – codes must be easily usable, capable of expansion and unambiguous (for a full discussion of coding see Chapter 5). A *location code* is probably the most suitable for this application, on, say, a 'Function – System – Unit' basis; e.g. E-03-01, where:

E = Engine (Function or possibly Department).

03 = Cooling water (System).

01 = Pump (Unit).

The code could later be further expanded to a fourth set of digits to identify components or maintenance tasks on that unit. It is also a good idea to tag the actual equipment with this code for identification on site.

The next stage is to establish, for each item of equipment, the factors relevant to the choice of maintenance policy for

25

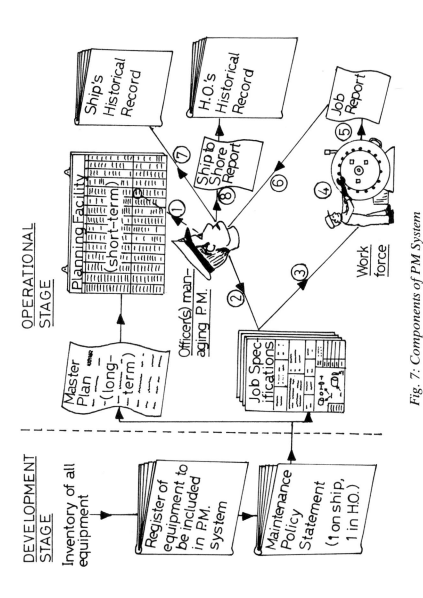

Fig. 7: Components of PM System

OPERATIONAL STAGE

Ship's Historical Record

H.O.'s Historical Record

Job Report

Ship to Shore Report

Planning Facility
(short-term)

Officer(s) managing P.M.

Master Plan
-(long-term)

Job Specifications

Work force

DEVELOPMENT STAGE

Inventory of all equipment

Register of equipment to be included in P.M. system

Maintenance Policy Statement
(1 on ship, 1 in H.O.)

that item. Probably the most important thing to consider here is the equipment's priority, i.e. its relative importance to the overall operation. Is it essential? If it is, preventive maintenance is likely to be most suitable. If it is not essential, perhaps breakdown maintenance is the most economic choice. However, there are other important factors which must be taken into account at this stage, e.g. spares availability, replacement cost, legal and classification requirements.

We are now in a position to select all the equipment to be included in the p.m. system and thus compile the register. Each item should be listed, ideally accompanied by all relevant technical information, such as manufacturer's performance specifications and spares details. Generally, more than one copy of this register is required, say one for head office and one for the ship. It must also be filed or compiled in such a way that information is easily retrievable.

Maintenance Policy Statement. In the register we have listed, for each item of equipment, the factors relevant to our choice of maintenance policy for that item. We must now weigh those factors and state our choice, always trying to keep the item we are considering 'in perspective' with regard to the overall maintenance resources and total operation to which it contributes. For example a piece of equipment although contributing to an essential operation is, in the short term, strictly non-essential because the operation could continue, though perhaps not so effectively, without it. (A mooring winch could fall into this category, provided there was another at the same end of the vessel which could be used). Spares for this item could be held aboard ship at reasonable cost. In this case, one might decide on a breakdown policy with minimum statutory and classification surveys and basic servicing (lubrication, etc.)

Having 'fitted' a suitable policy to each item, it is now necessary to identify the maintenance tasks needed to carry these policies through, and when they should be carried out. In the case of breakdown policies, maintenance, other than basic servicing, is carried out when failure occurs. In the case of preventive maintenance, one must decide on task frequencies, on a running or calendar time basis in the case of scheduled maintenance, or the condition or level of performance when maintenance should be carried out, in the case of maintenance based on monitoring.

When breaking down the maintenance work into the actual tasks themselves, several points have to be considered. Firstly, maintenance work should be combined with the necessary surveys wherever possible. If, say, a piece of machinery must be stripped down for a classification survey then, in most cases, this is the most sensible time to carry out any necessary maintenance, rather than having to strip it down again a short time later. In fact, many preventive p.m. schedules are based on survey requirements. One must also consider the size, order and grouping of these tasks, and the best times (apart from survey considerations) to carry them out. Such factors as weather conditions, port time, necessary availability of equipment and manpower must be taken into account here. If time in port does not normally exceed two days, it would be unwise to state a three day in-port task. Very often it is easier to run several tasks in parallel, if, for example, they all involve taking the same system out of service.

Resources, i.e. men, spares and maintenance equipment are important. With regard to men, suitable skill levels and the necessary number should prevail. As to equipment and spares, these must be available on board or, if the task is to be done in port, easily obtainable from ashore. Skilled or unskilled labour might also be obtainable ashore and tasks involving their work could be included in the statement. There is no reason why the system cannot include maintenance carried out by persons other than the ship's crew.

Finally, the time that each task should take must be considered. There are several approaches to this problem. One is *work study*, i.e. studying the task being carried out, identifying the most efficient procedure and estimating the time it should take using various predetermined standards. Another approach is to analyse the data from previous reports of the same or similar task. This is acceptable provided first of all that such records have been accumulated, and that ineffi-ciencies – probably not mentioned in the reports – can be identified. A further alternative, and perhaps the most logical, is to consult those who have experience in supervising and carrying out the task. Information achieved in this way is extremely useful but should not always be accepted without question, since it is subject to individuals' opinions, which may vary. Whichever approaches are adopted, one must con-sider the equipment and materials used for the job, the skill levels of those involved, the state of the item on which the job is being carried out, and the conditions under which those involved must work (e.g. temperature, up-hand or down-hand work).

Different views are held on exactly what the time should represent. Should it be a 'target' time, i.e. an ideal time, or a more realistic expected time? The answer to this one is in the attitude of the work force. If they are likely to try to work towards a target time, then give them that time on the Job Specification. If it is likely to offend, then it is probably not such a good idea. Also, a realistic expected time to complete the job is more useful for planning purposes.

When stating the tasks in this document then, the fol-lowing should be included, for each task:

(i) Identification of task (the location code could be applied here, Function-System-Unit-Task).

(ii) Full description.

(iii) Maintenance equipment required.

(iv) Spares required.

(v) Men required (number and skill levels).

(vi) Time to complete the task.

(vii) Task frequency or state of equipment/equipment's performance when task to be undertaken.

The layout and compilation of this information should lend itself to updating.

This document is essential to those responsible for long-term planning and, like the register, one copy would normally be held in head office, another aboard ship although (assuming the tasks are described in sufficient detail in the Job Specifications and a Master Plan is provided (see below)) it need not be referred to frequently and is there more in the form of back-up information.

We now move to the p.m. 'operating' components, which enable the policies and tasks, stated in the Policy Statement, to be followed through.

Job Specifications. These are variously known by such titles as Job Cards, Work Orders, Work Information Cards and Maintenance Guides, but basically they are the means of communicating the necessary information about the maintenance tasks to those who will actually carry out these tasks. They usually take the form of a breakdown of the tasks in the Policy Statement, very often one Job Specification per task (sometimes the bulk of the Policy Statement is in fact a comprehensive set of the Job Specifications).

Each Job Specification should show the task information listed in the Policy Statement, but presented in a manner easily understandable to the persons for whom it is intended, plus any extra information on actually carrying out the work that might be helpful. This could range from a 'blow by blow' description of how to perform the task, to references to manuals should a problem arise. Sometimes this type of information is a result of work study techniques being applied to tasks, the order of the different operations involved in a task becoming important. A caution, though, on task descriptions or instructions. They should never insult the intelligence of those who are to use them. If they do, they might well cause a feeling of contempt for the system in the minds of the work force. At the other extreme, the job instructions should not be too complex for the man to understand. One view held is that a full account of the work to be done on the Job Specification is, provided it is followed, a form of 'insurance policy' for the maintainer, since should a failure occur shortly after an overhaul, he can rightly claim that he is not to blame. However, this view is, in the author's opinion, not one which will encourage a responsible attitude to maintenance work. In any event, it is very important that the reasons for including, on the Job Specifications, comprehensive job descriptions or instructions should be made clear to the work force, along with the intended attitude with which they should view them (e.g. the information is only there for them to refer to if they need it). If this is done, the work force, once they have got used to them, will generally find them helpful, and they can be particularly useful on ships with general purpose crews. The level of maintenance expertise of such crews in some areas is often quite low and Job Specifications, carrying clear instructions, can compensate for this to some extent.

Job Specifications, since they are intended to be handled by those doing the job, often on site, are usually printed on card or paper which is subsequently sealed in plastic coating. Normally they are filed away until required but sometimes are used as planning cards or placed in wallets which also contain Job Report forms (mentioned later). In some p.m. systems, the Job Specifications include a section for the maintainer to make a brief report (spares used, defects found, etc.). This report can be recorded when returned to, say, the Chief Engineer and, assuming the Job Specification is plastic covered, he can then simply erase it and return it to the file.

Master Plan (Long-term). Obviously, maintenance work cannot be planned to an indefinite period ahead, and some time span must be decided upon as the long-term planning period. Often, with ship-board p.m. systems, this time span approximates to the interval of time between dry-docks and ideally should be easily divisible into short-term planning periods, which usually correspond to voyage length, e.g. 5 years divided into twenty 3 month periods.

The Master Plan is a plan of the work to be undertaken over the long-term period, i.e. a 'plan of attack' devised by those responsible for long-term planning, usually at head office but possibly shipboard personnel. It should be available on the ship at the start of the period. The Plan itself may take several forms. If the majority of work is preventive scheduled maintenance, which at the present time it usually is, then the Plan may lay down a schedule for all the work in the period. The schedule should not be too rigid at this stage, since it is

31

impossible to plan accurately over, say, five years. One simply cannot know all the things that will happen to a ship over such a long period of time. To avoid excessive rigidity, the Master Plan could, for example, simply list (but not schedule) all tasks which have a frequency inside the short-term period, leaving these tasks to be planned in detail by shipboard personnel. It could roughly schedule tasks with frequencies outside the short-term period, allowing shipboard personnel to fit them into that period where most convenient.

Maintenance based on running time is difficult to plan, however one should have a reasonable idea of equipment usage and therefore be able to draw up an approximate projection of the maintenance work on this equipment to include in the Master Plan.

For preventive maintenance based on monitoring a schedule of actual maintenance work cannot be laid down, but a monitoring programme of the relevant equipment could be mapped out in the Master Plan.

On equipment where a breakdown policy has been adopted one can only consider routine servicing for scheduling and, again, attempt to make a projection of probable breakdown work over the long-term planning period so that, firstly, it will not seriously disrupt other planned work and, secondly, adequate resources (i.e. men, equipment, spares) will be available.

Basically, then, the Master Plan is a concerted plan of maintenance work on all equipment included in the p.m. system for the long-term planning period. One could liken it to an orchestral arrangement. The tasks stated in the Policy Statement are like the musical lines of each instrument, the Master Plan the orchestral score, bringing together and harmonising the music of each instrument for the best effect.

Planning Facility (Short-term). If the Master Plan is a detailed plan over the long-term period, and can be kept to, then one could argue that no further planning was necessary. However, as has already been said, such a Master Plan is not generally advisable unless the period is short. It is better not to make the

Master Plan too specific 'time-wise', but to leave detailed planning till nearer the date. This is achieved by using a Planning Facility for detailed planning of the short-term period. It may, in fact, be divided into several facilities, each one progressively more short-term and detailed. For example, if the short-term period is 3 months, one could have a 3 month plan, planning to the nearest week, and another plan spanning a week planning, perhaps, to the nearest hour.

The Planning Facility would, of course, be carried on board the ship (although there may be another in head office, updated whenever reports are received from the ship) and the planning, at least during the voyage, handled by those ship-board personnel responsible for the operation of the p.m. system. Hence it must have one very important feature; it must be flexible, i.e. one must be able to actually plan with it to the detail required. It should also be possible to amend the plan when necessary; e.g. it must accommodate unplanned breakdowns and defect work, or planned work which for some reason must be carried over to a later date. Often some sort of job priority system is desirable to effectively achieve this. If this cannot be accomplished then a backlog of work is the most common result. It should be said, however, that while a backlog is not, in the main, desirable it can be tolerated if at some period, probably during dry-docking, time and resources are given to clearing it.

There are several purposes of the Planning Facility. The first is, as mentioned, to allow detailed short-term planning. The second is to give an overall 'picture' of the maintenance work in the short-term planning period, at any stage during this period – both the work already done and that still to be done. This allows one to easily assess 'the state of the game', as it were, helping to assess men, spares and equipment required, aiding future planning (possibly into the next short-term period), and serving as an immediate reminder of the maintenance work to be done. Thirdly, it enables maintenance work to be fitted in with other operations going on aboard the ship. It is most important that one should always be aware of these operations while planning maintenance, both from the point of view of the correct use of manpower and from that of ensuring that the equipment (the maintenance of which one is responsible for) is always available for essential operations when required.

The actual form taken by the Planning Facility varies. It may take the form of a chart, preferably with some method of erasing for re-planning etc. However, this system is not very flexible and one must constantly refer to another document, possibly the Master Plan, to remind oneself of the tasks, and also their code if this is to be entered on the chart.

Planning boards with either planning cards or wallets (containing, say, job specifications and job reports) are very popular, as these give a good visual display of the work load and are easy to plan with if they are carefully designed. Planning cards are often a different colour on each side so that when a job is completed they can be turned round, thus showing at a glance work done and work outstanding. The board itself may be divided into vertical columns, each column representing say one week, with slots to take the cards, breaking the week up into periods of a day. There are, in fact, several different arrangements of this type in common use at sea.

Filing systems are another alternative though, in the author's experience, these do not offer such a good visual display as boards and are not so easy to plan with. They also tend to be rather 'fiddley'. There are several different types of systems in existence, e.g. troughs containing cards or book-type loose leaf files.

Sometimes the Planning Facility may be a combination of the above types, e.g. a chart covering the whole short-term planning period, with a planning board for detailed planning of each week's workload. Generally speaking, the Facility should be tailored to the detail of planning required, the type of person using it and the time available to make use of it. It must fulfil its intended purposes, mentioned above, particularly with regard to its ability to be used to actually plan, as well as display the work load.

To summarise, if we likened the Master Plan to an orchestral score, we could liken the Planning Facility to the conductor. He interprets the score and continuously co-ordinates the efforts of the individual players. The Planning Facility should be used to interpret the Master Plan in greater detail and to co-ordinate the tasks on a continuous basis.

Reporting System. Reporting on maintenance work is important for two reasons. Firstly, those in control of p.m. must be informed that work has or has not been done, or needs to be done. This enables them to monitor the progression of the plan, i.e. keep their Planning Facility up to date, and hence exert short-term control. Secondly, records should be kept (and to compile records one must receive reports) for subsequent reference and analysis, facilitating long-term control of the p.m. system.

Reporting is the means of 'feedback' from those actually carrying out the maintenance to all those controlling the p.m. system, both ashore and afloat. There are two reporting channels, one within the ship, the other from ship to shore. The type of report going through these channels may, in fact, be the same in the case of the maintainers completing Job Reports and passing them to the officer responsible for p.m. in their department (the Chief Engineer or Chief Officer). He, having noted the information, forwards them to the head office. Alternatively, the Chief Engineer or Chief Officer may extract only the details from the job reports that head office require and, perhaps together with other comments and information, compose a separate periodical report of his own. He may, in fact, only report to head office information concerning maintenance work done, or required, which falls outside the requirements of the p.m. system (known as 'by exception' reporting), thus reducing the amount of reporting necessary.

Reporting within the ship, i.e. Job Reports from the maintainers to the officers responsible for p.m. may, as mentioned earlier, be achieved via the returned Job Specifications, or via a separate Job Report form or, in a simple system, by word of mouth. Whichever method is used, the following information should generally be included:

(i) Work completed.
(ii) Work which was not completed and the reasons why.

(iii) Defects discovered and whether they were corrected or not.

(iv) Spares used.

(v) Time taken.

(vi) Any general observations.

With regard to reporting from the ship to head office, it is difficult to state categorically what should and should not be reported since this will depend on the type of p.m. system adopted and the level of responsibility for maintenance given to shipboard staff. However, it is possible to make three general comments. Firstly, the ship should only include in the report – and head office should only ask for – information that will be useful for future reference and analysis in head office. Secondly, head office should not ask for information which it is impossible for the ship to supply or which it is more difficult for the ship to obtain than head office, particularly with regard to various manufacturers' codes, etc. Thirdly, standardised report forms are generally preferable for ship to shore reporting (rather than a 'letter' type of report) stating clearly what information is required. The ship's office then knows precisely what is required of him, and head office will receive exactly the information they require without wasting the officer's time supplying surplus information.

P.M. Records. There are two types of recording to be carried out. Firstly, such information, contained in the reports from the maintainers, necessary in order to exert short-term control; e.g. a planned task has or has not been successfully completed, or a particular task necessary to put right a defect needs to be planned. This form of recording need only involve updating or modifying the Planning Facility.

Secondly, we must build up a historical record for subsequent analysis, in order to discover whether the plan, and the equipment, are operating as well as they might and what modifications, if any, are necessary. For example comparison of recorded time taken to complete a job and planned time could lead to conclusions relating to the efficiency of the maintainers, the Job Specification or the piece of equipment.

We also need this historical record for reference purposes, e.g. checking what spares have been used on a particular piece of machinery, or how long the last overhaul of a particular item took. Basically, the historical record aids long-term control. It may be kept ashore or on the ship, or possibly both – each recording only such information as will be useful to them. Keeping records ashore has the added advantage of extending the possibilities of analysis, since analysing facilities (staff, computers, etc.) are more extensive than aboard ship and also inter-vessel comparison across the fleet may be carried out.

It may be thought necessary to add other information to that gleaned from the ship's reports in the compilation of the historical record, such as the costing of spares and labour, in order to aid analysis.

There are several different recording systems which may be adopted. Record cards, stored in troughs or files, are widely used or, on a more sophisticated level, computer data banks. The advantage of the latter method is that standard analysis programmes may be developed, producing, say, monthly analysis of costs, maintenance man-hours and so on. An automatic spares re-ordering system (assuming spares used on all tasks are reported and recorded) may even be based on this. The cost of such computer methods is expensive, although the growing influence of 'mini' computers is likely to dramatically reduce the cost.

The historical record is usually based around different items of equipment, i.e. a record is built up of each major item, or possibly a group of similar items, or items forming one system.

There are several features which any recording system must possess. Firstly, only information which is going to be used must be recorded. Secondly, this information must be easily stored. Thirdly, and most important, the information must be easily retrievable. Finally, it should easily yield trends and comparisons, thus making analysis of the information it contains as quick and as simple as possible.

Chapter 3
Spares Control

3.1 *Importance*

An efficient spares control system is vital to shipboard maintenance management. This point cannot be over-stressed. A planned maintenance system, involving either breakdown or preventive policies or both, requires adequate spares, at the right times, if it is to be successful. Conversely, it is impossible to estimate which spares to order in advance and in what numbers, unless maintenance is planned. In short, p.m. systems and spares systems are complementary, each needing the other. They should be closely knit, the spares system ideally forming an integral part of the p.m. system. If this is the case, the spares system will be designed, and will serve the maintenance operation, in the best way. Also, codes which are common to the p.m. system and the spares system can be used and documentation, in the form of reports, records, etc. can be greatly simplified. Cross-referencing between, for example, a maintenance task on a piece of equipment and the spares items required becomes much simpler.

It is, therefore, impossible to isolate the benefits of a good spares system from those of a good p.m. system, since the two are interdependant. Continuity (set against crew changes), economic savings, etc. are all benefits of both systems, but are not fully achieved unless both systems exist.

3.2 *Objectives*

The prime objectives of a spares control system are two-fold. Firstly, it must ensure that the 'right' amount of spares are held aboard ship. Secondly, it must ensure the availability of spares, when required, at the lowest cost. These objectives are inter-related since the choice of which spares to carry and in what numbers depends on what spares will be required. Spares stock (including consumable items such as paint, grease, packing, cleaning materials, etc.) carried aboard ship represent capital. If it is all used regularly, all well and good. If it is 'just sitting there' it becomes, in effect, 'dead money'. However, it has been stated earlier that it is impossible to eliminate the risk of breakdowns, no matter how preventive one's policy is, and one may decide to carry certain spares as insurance against a costly breakdown; e.g. a ship's spare anchor. Thus a balance must be found between the spares necessary to ensure the effectiveness of a maintenance policy and the cost of carrying these spares. If the stock level is too high, money is being wasted; too low and breakdown of maintenance policy, excessive downtime and high costs may result.

Broadly speaking, for items covered by a preventive policy, there must be sufficient spares to cover all planned work plus any breakdowns which might reasonably be expected. For items covered by a breakdown policy, spares carried should generally tend to be more extensive.

We should consider, when deciding on the extent of spares carried aboard ship, the availability of spares in the ship's ports of call. If adequate spares are easily and quickly available at a reasonable cost it may, in some cases, be advantageous to rely on obtaining the spares from these ports when required, rather than carrying them aboard for long periods. The possibilities of spares depots strategically placed around a shipping company's area of operation, flying certain high cost spares items out to the ship, or simply managing without the item in question until the home port is reached, should also be borne in mind.

3.3 Components

We are now going to look at the components of a shipboard spares control system (see Figure 8) in a similar way to that in which we looked at the p.m. system components – first the development stage and then the operational stage, then consider the physical aspect of the system, i.e. storekeeping, to get a complete picture. This will be dealt with in the next section.

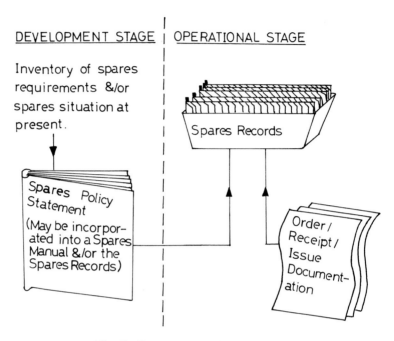

DEVELOPMENT STAGE | OPERATIONAL STAGE

Inventory of spares requirements &/or spares situation at present.

Spares Records

Spares Policy Statement
(May be incorporated into a Spares Manual &/or the Spares Records)

Order / Receipt / Issue Documentation

Fig. 8: Components of Spares System

First, then, the development stage. As with p.m., the first move is to take an inventory of all the spares requirements and their consumption rates (assuming that we are considering a comprehensive system, this also includes paint, cleaning materials, lubrication, etc). This information must come mainly from knowledge of the ship in question and her equipment, from the manufacturers and, if there is one, the p.m. system. Also, if a spares system is being installed on an existing ship rather than a new one, it is necessary to take an inventory of spares already held on board. The safest way to do this is to actually go on board and physically check it rather than relying on the ship's records (which might be subject to a time lapse and certain 'safety margins' built in by those on

40

board!) Having completed the necessary inventories we are now in the position to draw up the first component.

Spares Policy Statement. Before proceeding further, it is necessary to state the 'ground rules'. The Policy Statement may not, in the final system, appear as a separate document. It could very well be incorporated into the structure of the Spares Records or take the form of a spares manual.

It should basically lay down what spares are to be included in the system, how many to be held in stock aboard ship and when to re-order. It has already been decided what spares to consider at the inventory stage, so the problem now is to decide how many, if any, should be carried aboard. The question of when and how many to re-order is linked to this, since the level of any individual item held in stock will fluctuate as it is used and re-ordered. Thus, what we must determine are *maximum*, *minimum* and *re-order* stock levels. In practice, minimum and re-order stock levels are usually combined into one level, i.e. the level to which stock must fall before it is re-ordered, account having been taken of the fact that it may fall further before the re-ordered stock arrives at the ship. With regard to the number to be re-ordered, this is usually the difference between maximum and re-order levels; for example, for a particular item, maximum level = 6, re-order level = 2, nothing is done until stock level aboard ship falls to 2, when 4 more are re-ordered.

These levels for each item may be decided by such factors as:

(i) The demands of the p.m. system.

(ii) The risks and subsequent costs of a breakdown, which might need the spares item in question to rectify it.

(iii) The usage rate.

(iv) The time interval between the ship ordering and receiving the item.

(v) The cost.

(vi) The availability abroad.

(vii) Voyage length.

(viii) The availability of alternatives.

Such factors may be drawn from several sources, such as:

(i) The p.m. Policy Statement.
(ii) The p.m. Records (if the ship is new, the p.m. or spares records of a 'sister' ship may be helpful).
(iii) Manufacturers.
(iv) The experience of both shore and sea staff.

If these levels, and the amounts to re-order, are made absolutely clear to shipboard personnel and the spares ordering department, there should be no credibility gap between the two. In the absence of such a system, what can often happen is that shipboard personnel will over-order in the fear that when the order is received ashore the spares department will deem it too large and cut it back. In other words, a certain amount of distrust can exist between the two owing to the fact that neither have clear instructions as to exactly what is expected of them.

The Policy Statement must also clearly identify each spares item with regard to its use and for the purposes of re-ordering. This is normally done by using codes. A location code (see 2.3), i.e. Function-System-Unit-Component, is most suitable for identifying its use but has a distinct short-coming when it comes to re-ordering. It is not suitable for bulk ordering, since one type of item (e.g. an 'O' ring) may be a component of several different pieces of equipment, or even systems, and therefore may have more than one location code. If, say, six of this item need to be re-ordered, several location codes might have to be stated by the ship. However, if that item was identified by a separate spares ordering code, only one code number would need to be stated. Also, a manufacturer will supply a part which is in fact produced by another manufacturer for him. By building up data on the original sources of parts and also on parts which are common to several pieces of equipment, it is possible for a company's spares department to allocate spares ordering code numbers to each type of part. This enables the company to order from original, or 'source', manufacturers, which is easier for bulk ordering of particular parts by the spares department, while probably obtaining a financial saving as well as a saving in time.

Thus, a spares ordering code could be included to good effect in the Policy Statement. Manufacturers' own codes could also be included, but generally they are not recommended for use by ship's staff when re-ordering through the spares department ashore, as these codes often give rise to errors and ambiguities. It is usually better to leave the shore staff to translate items into these codes (possibly by computer) before ordering from the manufacturers.

Moving now to the operational stage, we have the following components.

Spares Records. It is essential that all spares movements are recorded. These records must be kept up to date and the information they contain should be readily available. It makes the job of re-ordering and controlling stock much easier for shipboard personnel if the relevant information from the Policy Statement is incorporated, per item, into these records; i.e. identification (including location code and, if there is one, spares ordering code) and maximum and re-ordering levels. They should also show, per item, present stock levels and outstanding orders to be delivered, preferably with the dates when the orders were made. Thus existing stock levels, items for re-ordering and numbers required, can all be drawn from these records.

The records should also lend themselves to analysis. It should be possible to tell whether the usage rates and delivery times are as predicted. If not, perhaps the maximum and re-order levels should be adjusted. Analysis could also show turn-over rates. If turn-over is unusually high, this probably indicates either a faulty (or inadequate) spare, or a weakness in the equipment of which it is a component. Increasing turn-over rates could indicate equipment deterioration, whereas reducing or very low turn-overs could indicate obsolescence – either of the spares or of the equipment.

Regular appraisal of spares costs can also be useful as a guide to the spares system's, and the equipment's, performances, as well as helping to make the crew more cost

43

conscious – assuming this information is imparted to them.

The power of analysis can be greatly improved by carrying out inter-ship comparisons. The trends for the fleet and variations of individual ships from the norm can then be seen. Also, combining spares and p.m. information for analysis, besides showing whether the two systems are complementing each other satisfactorily, allows more accurate and extensive analysis results.

As in the case of p.m. records, there are several different types of information storage suitable for spares records, but loose-leaf folders or troughs containing record cards are fairly common aboard ship. Whatever system is adopted, the emphasis should be on ease of use, i.e. quickness of both entering and extracting the desired information without error.

Often duplicate records for each ship are also held ashore and are up-dated as orders are received, stock sent to the ship, or periodical spares movements reports from the ship, devised for this purpose, are received. In most cases where records are held ashore, the reason is for analysis purposes only, but sometimes it is to remove the task of spares ordering from the ship (see 'automatic' spares ordering below). This type of information storage and analysis can be greatly facilitated by the use of a computer, standard programmes giving analysis information, say, every month.

Order/Receipt/Issue Documentation. There are three basic avenues of communication concerning the movement of spares and associated documentation:

(i) Between the spares department ashore and the manufacturers.

(ii) Between the ship and the spares department.

(iii) Within the ship.

Since we are interested in shipboard spares control systems, the main concern here is with the last two. In a special case a ship may order direct from a manufacturer, say in a foreign port, but this is rare and is usually done through the company's agent in that port, who is really acting, in this respect, as a representative of the company's spares department.

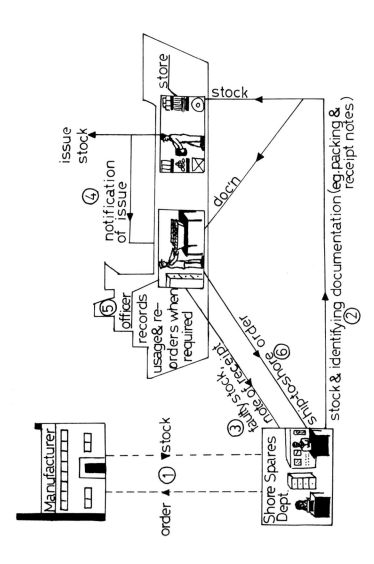

Fig. 9: Spares Stock and Documentation Flow

Spares Control

Spares documentation flow systems within the ship-to-shore channel vary widely, but the flow often roughly follows that shown in Figure 9. The spares department order spares from the manufacturers, to the fleet's requirements, and direct it to the ships, often marshalling the bulk of the main spares requirements together for one main delivery to a ship between voyages. Together with these spares go the necessary identifying documentation, e.g. packing and receipt notes. The ship will normally acknowledge receipt by returning the checked receipt notes and will record the delivered spares in the Spares Records. Faulty spares etc. would, where possible, be returned. Each spares item should also be readily identifiable, say by a tag attached to it, on arrival at the ship and during storage aboard.

As spares are issued from the ship's store, the responsible officer should be informed. This could be done by the storekeeper removing the tags from the spares on issue and delivering them periodically to the officer. Alternatively, the officer may be able to obtain the information from the maintenance work reports. The storekeeper may even be the officer responsible in some cases. In any event, the officer records the usage of spares in the Spares Records and, when the re-order level is reached on any item he indents for the appropriate number to bring the level back up to maximum. The re-ordering of items which are not urgent is often done at one time, say once per voyage.

The construction of the order form, requisition form, indent sheet, or whatever the company call the re-ordering medium between ship and shore, is very important. It should be a standardised form making it absolutely clear what information is required. There should be no room for ambiguities, particularly with regard to the various codes required; e.g. if a code number is asked for, is this the company's own spares ordering code or the manufacturer's code and, if it is the latter, which one, drawing number, serial number or some other? The form should be as simple as possible and, like p.m. reports, it should never ask for information which it is impossible to obtain aboard the ship, or is more difficult to obtain aboard than it would be for the spares department

46

ashore. It should be easy to complete, and should not, for example, demand that entries be typed (by an officer probably not skilled in typing) while not designed to facilitate this. It should also be possible to enter an adequate number of separate orders on one form.

Various 'automatic' spares ordering systems are also possible; i.e. the shore staff monitor and control the stock levels, rather than the ships' staff who simply inform the spares department ashore of spares usage. This information could be extracted from p.m. reports, or possibly the spares' identification tags, or a section of them, removed as the spares are issued and periodically returned to the spares department ashore, who then deduce what spares are required. Apart from some practical snags, such as tags becoming parted from their spares in transit or in store, in this latter system the whole concept of spares control from ashore has several serious disadvantages. Firstly, it does not generally encourage a responsible attitude of sea staff towards spares. Secondly, it is more difficult for shore staff to closely control the spares, because they cannot actually 'see' them and carry out physical inventories; also a time lag usually exists between a ship using spares and the shore knowing of it. Finally, considerable recording and ordering facilities are necessary ashore for these systems, often involving the use of computers.

3.4 *Storekeeping*

The physical aspect of storekeeping may be divided into *receiving*, *storage* and *issuing*.

Receiving. The storekeeper must check that everything entering his store is identifiable and is what is purports to be. He should also check the condition of the received items and, if they are not satisfactory, return them or record the faults.

Storage. Items should be stored so that they remain in good condition (dry, secured where necessary, etc). Pilfering of spares should be guarded against by ensuring that the shipboard stores are secure, and sensible security procedures devised and adhered to. All items should be stowed so that they can be easily retrieved when required. This calls for careful planning of storage space, especially since such space is often limited on a merchant vessel.

Stocktaking. Periodic inventories should be carried out to ensure that the actual stock levels agree with the records.

Issuing. Issuing spares is an important function of store-keeping. The storekeeper must ensure that the correct spares are issued for each job, all issues are authorised and, most important, all issues are reported or recorded so that the movement of spares stock is known.

Chapter 4
System Types

4.1 *Options*

Once a shipping company have made the conscious decision to adopt planned maintenance aboard their ships, they are faced with several options.

Firstly, they may develop their own system. To do this they must first realise and quantify their problems, limiting factors and objectives (see Chapter 1). If they do not, they will end up with a system which will not be ideally suited to their own operation and ships. They should also try to bring themselves abreast of the 'state of the art'. This is not always easy since these systems are a saleable commodity and as such are cloaked in a certain amount of secrecy. However, the techniques and facilities involved (with regard to documentation, coding, reporting and recording, spares ordering, planning, computer applications and so on) should be studied. In short, the company must often start at or near the bottom of the learning curve.

Secondly, a consultancy firm may be sought. Systems from these firms, although not particularly cheap, are based on a certain amount of past experience – depending, of course, upon which firm is approached. They will usually either design a system from scratch, to a customer's specification (subject to advice from the consultants), or supply 'off the peg' modules of planning systems, manuals, reporting systems, spares systems, etc., made up into a maintenance management package approximately suitable to the customer's set of criteria. Some consultants offer to handle the system after installation (recording, analysing, spares ordering, etc). No consultant, however, should instal a system and then wash his hands of it. He should always return to assess it after a reasonable period, say a year, and modify it as necessary.

The third option is to purchase a management system from another shipping company. There are several companies which have their own technical services divisions, operating rather like consultants. The disadvantage of doing this is that the systems which they are offering have most probably been designed for their own ships, and may not be entirely suitable for other company's.

Finally, a shipping company may decide not to adopt any formal system at all, but leave maintenance management more or less totally in the hands of shipboard personnel, possibly just handling spares requisitions and de-briefing at the ends of voyages. This is not without merit under the right circumstances, since personnel job satisfaction, and hence motivation, in these conditions can be great. However, if this philosophy is adopted it is imperative that the personnel on board responsible for the maintenance should have the ability, i.e. sufficient maintenance management experience and training, to carry it out. Even then, generally, it is preferable to provide personnel with the framework and hardware of a system to work with, albeit a simple one. In any event, there should be adequate communication between ship and shore staff so that both the maintenance management and maintenance work of sea staff can be adequately monitored, and sea staff can quickly and easily obtain information and advice from shore when they require it.

4.2   *System Examples*

Firstly let us look at some formal systems, i.e. systems devised by shipping companies, consultants or manufacturers. These systems will usually cover machinery, probably electrical equipment, deck equipment and possibly ship fabric (paintwork, etc). In the case of manufacturers, only their own equipment will be covered by their system. Rather than study the whole system of each example we will pick out the most interesting aspects.

Example A – Shipping Company. This company has approximately twenty ships engaged on a world wide trade. The voyage lengths are variable and the reliability of the ships must therefore be high. The p.m. system adopted by this company is, in essence, quite simple. It was built up around the Lloyd's five-year continuous survey cycle. Lloyd's requirements are included in the system plus any inspections, overhauls, etc., which the company think necessary, but the frequencies of these extra inspections and overhauls are kept to a minimum as it is felt that the Chief Engineer and First Mate on the ship are the best persons to decide when and where extra work is to be done. Thus more initiative is left with those on the ship and the system is flexible. The system can therefore be described as a simple overall plan from head office with detailed planning by shipboard personnel.

The Chief Engineer and First Mate operate the p.m. system aboard ship in their respective departments and handle the documentation. Neither is in overall charge. The Master is consulted when required, but is not usually involved. (This particular company differs from most other companies, where the Chief Engineer is in overall charge of the system). The Second Engineer also assists, mainly with spare parts control.

The p.m. system is based on calendar time, although there is nothing to prevent the Chief Engineer from using running time on certain items where it is possible to do so and is felt preferable. A small number do this. It is suspected that, on deck, calendar time is almost exclusively used.

The ship's contact is mainly with the shore based superintendents and the p.m. and spares departments in head office, although there may be the occasional need to contact manufacturers and outside contractors directly, but this is generally done by shore staff.

The p.m. system centres around the p.m. and record charts; p.m. charts are provided on each ship, with copies (for individual ships) kept in head office (see Figure 10). On each ship there are usually three charts, one for the engineering department, one for the deck department and one for the catering department. The electrical work is usually included

51

in the engineering chart with the exception of deck electrical equipment and navigational aids, etc. which are on the deck chart. Sometimes, however, a separate electrical department chart is provided. These charts show times for surveys, inspection, overhauls, etc. (including those required by DoT and classifications societies) and painting schemes. Each item included in the p.m. scheme is given a code number, which is

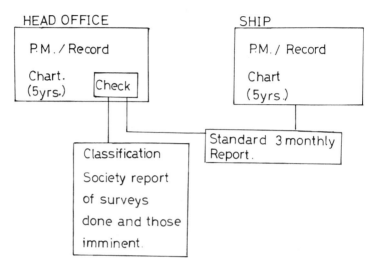

Fig. 10: PM Charts (Example 'A')

just a straight-forward numbering system rather than the logically devised location code, which would be more flexible, easier to interpret and reduce mistakes made. A colour code is also used on the p.m. charts, which cover a five year cycle, to indicate the time relative to the cycle at which, say, a survey should be carried out; the first year surveys are *brown*, the second year surveys *yellow*, etc. On the deck p.m. chart a diagramatic presentation (similar to a capacity plan) is also shown, mainly indicating different surveys.

Incorporated into the charts is a recording facility. The charts are simply divided into columns, each column representing three months. The Chief Engineer and First Mate mark work completed on their respective charts by indicating the number, colour code and a particular symbol indicating

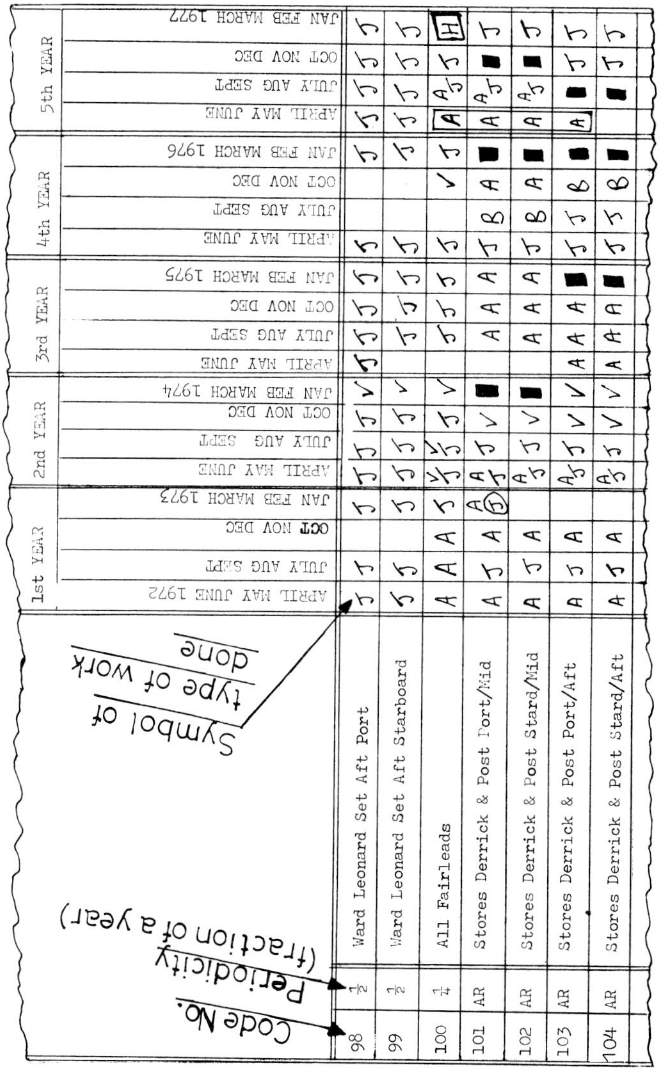

Fig. 11: Extract from PM Chart

the type of work done. Figure 11 shows a section of the deck p.m. chart;

AR = as required,
J = good condition,
P = poor,
√ = satisfactory,
Box round symbol = shore labour etc.

They then send in to the p.m. department in head office a summarised report, in the same code system, of p.m. work done approximately every three months on standardised report forms (see Figure 12). Dates shown are survey certificates expiry dates, last dry dock dates, date job last done, etc. (as specified on chart). Unplanned repair work and faults are reported separately as special reports to the superintendents. The standard p.m. reports are checked in head office, against classification society reports to the company on surveys done and those still outstanding, since discrepancies are not unknown. (Lloyds issue a regular computer print-out to companies, giving this information).

One important observation to make on this system is that the p.m. chart shows how often the work is to be done, and acts as a combined policy statement and master plan. No short-term planning facility is formally included in the system.

The spares system is a maximum/minimum one and is quite sophisticated, involving a fair amount of paper work. For each ship, there are two filing cabinets (each containing identical information), one kept in the superintendent's department in head office, the other in the Chief Engineer's office on board.

Spares on board are kept on numbered shelves or, for large items, stowage position is numbered. The documentation within each filing cabinet consists of the following four cards for each machine:

(i) *Data Sheet* (Figure 13). This shows a description of the machine, the manufacturer (together with address and telephone number), serial number, drawing number and part code number. The part code number is a type of location

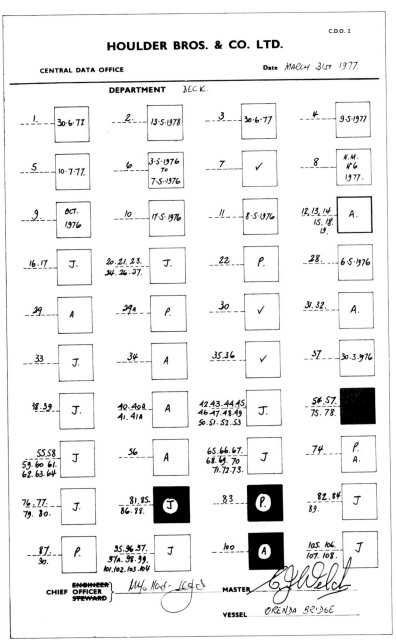

Fig. 12: Deck Report Form

DATA SHEET			
COMPONENT MAIN ENGINE.8 CYLINDER TWO-STROKE, SINGLE ACTING.			
SUB SYSTEM/SERVICE VALVE GEAR			
MANUFACTURER & ADDRESS H&W B&W HARLAND & WOLFF LTD. BELFAST			
		TEL. No. BELFAST 58456	
TYPE 8.K.98 FF	YEAR 1974	SERIAL No. 2645	
		DWG. No. ENGINE SKETCH 80900	
		MARK	
CAPACITY	WORKING PRESS	REVOLUTIONS	
H.P. INDICATED 30400	BORE 980 M/M	STROKE 2000 M/M	
METRIC			
OTHER DATA TURBO CHARGED ENGINE			
PRIME MOVER/MOTOR MANUFACTURER			
TYPE	SERIAL No.	DWG. No.	
H.P. R.P.M.	VOLTAGE	AMPS Hz.	
		RATING	
WIRING DATA			
TYPE OF BEARING	BUSH DATA		
STARTER PARTICULARS			
UNITS ON BOARD OF SAME TYPE			
GROUP MAIN ENGINE	DESIGNATION/SYSTEM VALVE GEAR	CODE 1/11	

Fig. 13: Data Sheet

code, e.g. 1/3/26, the 1 indicating main engine, the 3 indicating fuel system and the 26 indicating the line number on the particular section of the Inventory Sheet (this last number is not shown on the Data Sheet, since it refers to the whole machine, not individual parts listed line by line in the Inventory Sheet).

COMPONENT/SYSTEM. MAIN ENGINE			INVENTORY SHEET			
VALVE GEAR					CODE No. 1/11	
LINE No.	DESCRIPTION	ORDERING DATA	STORAGE LOCATION	STOCK MAX.	MIN.	PART CODE No.
1	KEY	0271	SHELF 10	2	1	1/11/1
2	ROCKER ARM SHAFT	0360	FLOOR 12	1	1	1/11/2
3	SCREWS	0459	SHELF 10	6	2	1/11/3
4	GASKET	0726	" 10	6	2	1/11/4
5	GASKET	0904	" 10	6	2	1/11/5
6	BUSH	4297	FLOOR 12	2	1	1/11/6
7						
8						
9						
10						
11						
12						

Fig. 14: Inventory Sheet

(ii) *Inventory Sheet* (Figure 14). This describes the spares held for the machinery on the Data Sheet, together with the manufacturer's ordering code, stowage location (shelf number, etc), maximum/minumum stock levels and part code number.

(iii) *Stock Record Card* (Figure 15). Entries are made on this card (in pencil and on the line number corresponding to that on the Inventory Sheet) when the stock level of a component falls below the maximum. If the stock level reaches the minimum, an order is sent to head office to bring the balance back up to maximum. An example of the entries where maximum = 6 and minimum = 2 is shown on Figure 15.

STOCK RECORD CARD										CODE No.					
MAIN ENGINE			COMPONENT/SYSTEM	VALVE GEAR						1/11					
LINE No.	DATE	USED / REC'D.	BAL.	DATE	USED / REC'D.	BAL.	DATE	USED / REC'D.	BAL.	DATE	USED / REC'D.	BAL.	DATE	USED / REC'D.	BAL.
3	2/75	-/6	6	4/75	4/-	2	6/75	-/4	6						
		Spares received			Order to Head Office			Spares received							

Fig. 15: Stock Record Card

(iv) *Follow-up Sheet* (Figure 16). Entries are made here, in pencil for easy deletion, whenever levels are below minimum, i.e. ordering is necessary, and when the components are received. Entries should be made on the correct line number.

To enable records and stock levels to be kept up-to-date, four sets of forms are used. These are as follows:

(i) *Amendment Sheet* (Figure 17). This sheet may be used by ship or head office when additional spare gear is introduced or when stock levels are changed. If sea staff think that,

COMPONENT/SYSTEM MAIN ENGINE VALVE GEAR														SPARE GEAR FOLLOW-UP SHEET CODE: 1/11					
LINE No.	DATE	ORDER QTY.	DATE	REC'D QTY.	DATE	ORDER QTY.	DATE	REC'D QTY.	DATE	ORDER QTY.	DATE	REC'D QTY.	DATE	ORDER QTY.	DATE	REC'D QTY.	DATE	ORDER QTY.	DATE	REC'D QTY.
1																				
2																				
3	4/15	4	6/15	4																
4																				
5																				
6																				
7																				
8																				
9																				
10																				
11																				
12																				

Fig. 16: Follow-up Sheet

say, a stock level should be changed they could complete an Amendment Sheet and send it to head office for approval. The sheet basically requires part code number, part description, stowage location and ordering number.

ADDITIONS/ALTERATIONS TO SPARE PART INVENTORY MACHINERY CONCERNED:				MV/SS. DATE PAGE No.		
EQUIP CODE No.	LINE No.	DESCRIPTION OF PART	STORAGE LOCATION	PART No. ORDERING DATA		NOTES
1/11	5	GASKET	SHELF 10	0904		

NOTES:

SHIP RECOMMENDS CHANGE OF STOCK LEVELS
FROM MAX 6 , MIN 2 ;
TO MAX 8 , MIN 3 .

SIGNED

CHIEF ENGINEER/SUPT. ENGINEER.

Fig. 17: Amendment Sheet

(ii) *Consumption Form* (Figure 18). Used aboard ship only, a pad being kept in stores ideally. A person taking an item should complete this form, which is then passed to the Chief Engineer who extracts the information from them at weekly intervals. Periodically these forms are sent to head office as a cross check for records. The forms require part code number, spares consumed, stock balance and date.

SPARE PART CONSUMPTION SHEET			PAGE No.			
			WEEK ENDING			
ITEM OF EQUIPMENT	SPARES CONSUMED	STOCK BALANCE	ITEM OF EQUIPMENT	SPARES CONSUMED	STOCK BALANCE
1 / 11 / 3	4	2			
TO BE RETURNED TO C/E BY SECOND ENGINEER WEEKLY					SPERRY REMINGTON LM124
			SIGNED		

Fig. 18: Consumption Sheet

(iii) *Report Form* (Figure 19). This is an annual report form, but it is advised that one third of the file should be covered every four months, or each time the Chief Engineer is relieved, and sent to head office. Information is extracted from the Stock Record Cards. The form requires date, part code number, consumption during last twelve months, and quantity in stock at time of check. There is also an additional consumption check column which can be completed if head office require a detailed watch on a particular item.

(iv) *Requisition Form* (Figure 20). This is an adapted version of the requisition form used prior to the introduction of the system. Entries must be typed. The form requires all details from the Data Sheet, i.e. manufacturer's address, machinery description, serial number, drawing number plus – for each part – quantity required, description, manufacturer's order number, quantity on board, part code number and dates when order sent and received, together with signatures. In emergencies part code numbers can be quoted by wireless telephone, and in these cases a special form is completed in the office with copies forwarded to the ship.

SPARE PART REPORT FORM

DATE:

SHIP: SS/MV.   PAGE No.

EQUIP. CODE No.	LINE No.	CONS. LAST 12 MONTHS	ACC. CONS.	QTY. IN STOCK	EQUIP CODE No.	LINE No.	CONS. LAST 12 MONTHS	ACC. CONS.	QTY. IN STOCK
1/11	1	2		2					
1/11	2	1		1					
1/11	3	4		6					
1/11	4	3		6					
1/11	5	6	2/VoyAGE	2					
1/11	6	1		1					

TO BE FORWARDED TO SUPT. DEPT. EVERY 12 MONTHS   SPERRY REMINGTON LMI19

SIGNED

CHIEF ENGINEER

Fig. 19: Report Form

Where deck equipment and machinery comes under the system, the senior deck officers are responsible for maintaining the records in co-operation with the Chief Engineer. The superintendents will also give all assistance possible, and run spot checks (never more than once a year) to check that the systems in particular ships are running as they should be.

⊕ Houlder Brothers & Co Ltd
53 Leadenhall Street London EC3A 2BR

13

No.

S/S
_____
M/S

REQUISITION FOR SPARES
PLEASE KEEP THIS COPY UPPERMOST WHEN TYPING

FOR OFFICE USE ONLY

FOR OFFICE USE ONLY

ACK.	
DLY.	
DES.	
A/C.	

STATE FULLY MANUFACTURERS NAME, DATA FROM NAMEPLATE

H.&W B.&W. HARLAND & WOLFF LTD ., BELFAST

MAIN ENGINE TYPE 8K 98 FF. SERIAL 2645

DRG.NO. 80900

Item No.	Quantity Required	Manufacturers Part Description & Part Number PLEASE ENTER DETAILS IN BLOCK LETTERS	Quantity on Board	REMARKS OR OWNERS CODE
	1	KEY 0271	1	1/11/1
	1	ROCKER ARM SHAFT, 0360	NIL	1/11/2

ORDER COMPLETED................19....... SIGNED.............................

SHIPS CONSECUTIVE No

ORDER RECEIVED AS TICKED	ORDER NOT RECEIVED
.............19....SIGNED............	..............19.....SIGNED............
.............19....SIGNED............	..............19.....SIGNED............
.............19....SIGNED.............	..............19.....SIGNED...........

_____Master/Chief Engineer

DATE _____

PORT _____

OFFICE USE

ORIGIN   DATE

Fig. 20: Requisition Form

Looking analytically at this system we can categorise the various pieces of documentation into the basic components as described in Chapter 3. The Data Sheet and the Inventory Sheet form the policy statement. The Stock Record Cards and the Follow-up Sheets form the recording systems. The Report Form is, of course, the means of reporting from ship to shore. The Requisition Form provides the necessary ordering and receipt documentation. The Consumption Form essentially provides the communication within the ship on the issue of spares. The Amendment Sheet provides an extra element of communication allowing the system to be kept up-to-date and improved upon.

Example B – Consultants. The company referred to here was one of the first firms of consultants in this field. The services which they offer are as follows:

(i) *Planned Maintenance Systems.* These systems are developed for specific vessels or classes of vessels, depending also on trading patterns, manning scales, company policy, etc., being – they claim – equally effective on new or existing ships. They also undertake improvement to existing maintenance systems. The usual type of system installed incorporates the use of planning boards which, if required, become part of a shipboard management system covering the total work load of the ship.

(ii) *Vibration Analysis.* This facility may be used in the development of p.m. systems to determine the priorities for maintenance. It is also available as a separate service if required, as a complete package including suitable equipment, training of operators and simple operating instructions on its use and the interpretation of readings.

(iii) *Stock Control.* They supply a simple card indexing system for storekeeping and an indenting facility, and they claim to be able to avoid the carrying of unnecessary spares items on ships.

(iv) *Operating Manuals.* These manuals can be produced to cover all ship operations. They may also be extended to contain maintenance information. They are based on Operational Sequence Diagrams (O.S.D.'s), fault-diagnosis charts, systems drawings, etc. They are advantageous over manufacturers' manuals in that the depth of coverage is even, and interfaces between associated pieces of equipment are covered.

(v) *Shipboard Management System Installation and Training.* This firm have developed a shipboard management system, i.e. a planning facility to enable a management team, composed of senior members of each department, to plan the day to day work load of all personnel aboard ship. If a comprehensive shipboard management system is installed, the p.m. becomes a part of it, although not necessarily the maintenance stock control.

The firm provides various management courses but runs special courses for senior shipboard personnel (and initially shore personnel who are involved) when shipboard management systems are installed on a company's ships. Figure 21 shows a member of a course engaged in a planning exercise on the planning boards provided by the firm.

Fig. 21: Exercise on Planning Boards

Work Information	**S.S. Esso** .....Hampshire.....	**Maker** 011	**System** 07	**Equip.** 02	**Item** 06.1

Work Source.	De-oiler No.1
Location.	Engine room Platform level, Port. Forward.
Work Description.	Cleaning and examination of float controlled air vents.
SAFETY Precautions.	Inlet and outlet valves shut and lashed.

No. of Men. 1	**Skill.** K1 EO	**Skill**	**Skill.**	**Target Time.** 2½ Hours.

Tools & Materials.

¼" Whit O.E. Spanner
⅜" Whit O.E. Spanner.
Wheelkey
De-greaseant liquid
Rags
Torch.

5 air vessel cover joints.

Method.

1. Shut and lash inlet and outlet valves.
2. Open top drain valves until flow ceases.
3. Remove nuts and cover from air vent vessel.
4. Remove and clean ball float, clean out air vent vessel.
5. Examine vent valve and vent valve seat for wear.
6. Check air escape passage is clear.
7. Check float for leakage (shake float to find out if there is water inside.
8. Check condition of air vessel cover joint, renew if damaged.
9. Replace ball float, air vessel cover joint, cover and nuts.

© 1969 S.S.Stevenson & Ptnrs.

Fig. 22: Work Information Card

METHOD

10. Repeat elements 4 to 10 for remaining air vents.

11. Open inlet valve.

12. Open top drain valves (c), close when water flows.

13. Open outlet valve to place de-oiler in service.

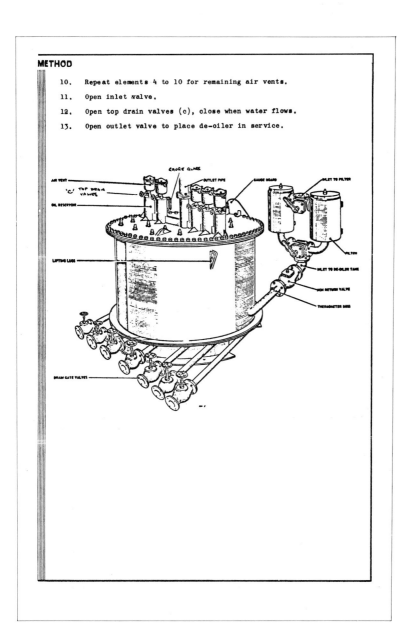

System Types

The firm in question has devised several systems; a typical one is considered here and it will be seen that it is quite sophisticated. Its documentation fairly closely follows the basic components as explained in Chapter 2. There is an Equipment Register, Policy Statement and Master Plan. The reporting and recording, while fairly detailed (the reports being on standardised forms), are of the 'by exception' type.

The most interesting parts, however, are the Job Specifications and Short-term Planning Facilities and it is on these aspects that we will concentrate. The Job Specifications consist of the following:

(i) *Work Information Cards (W.I.C's)* (see Figure 22). These show work source, location, work description, safety details, number of men required, skill levels (in a skill code) required, target time, tools and materials required, method, equipment code, item number and maker code.

(ii) *Operational Sequence Diagrams (O.S.D.'s)* (see Figure 23). To be used instead of W.I.C.'s where operation sequence diagrams are felt necessary, otherwise they show the same information as W.I.C.'s.

Equipment Code is a four-figure location code indicating system and equipment, e.g. 1501. 15 = Electrical Supply, 01 = Main Turbo Alternator. *Item Number* identifies a task while indicating its periodicity. A large job is broken down into reasonably sized tasks and each task then allocated a separate item number; e.g. 01.1 or 03.2, the first two numbers indicating once per month or once per three months respectively, and the third number indicating the first monthly task or the second three monthly task, respectively, on the piece of equipment being considered. *Maker Code* is simply a three figure number to identify different manufacturers. *Skill Code* is the code indicating the levels of skill required for different tasks. It consists of one letter and one number. The letters are 'K' for theoretical knowledge, or 'E' for practical experience. The numbers are 0 through to 3 for different levels of knowledge or experience; e.g. K0 = no theoretical knowledge of item considered, or E3 = complete familiarity of all tools and procedures connected with item considered.

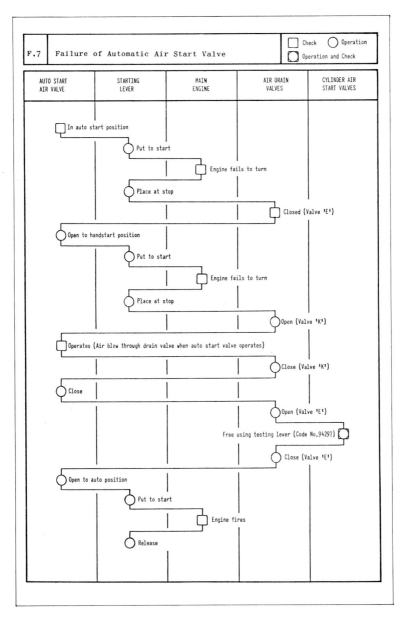

Fig. 23: Operational Sequence Diagram

System Types

The Short-term Planning Facilities can be itemised as follows:

(i) *Planning Cards.* One for each maintenance item, i.e. they show equipment code, item number, maker code, task description, skills required and target time; they also act as record cards, i.e. actual time taken and date completed can be entered (and erased when noted); these cards are moved to the planning boards as required.

(ii) *Defect Notes.* These are standard forms which are raised by the relevant officer stating the work necessary to put right any defect. They are placed either in the quarter or weekly plan.

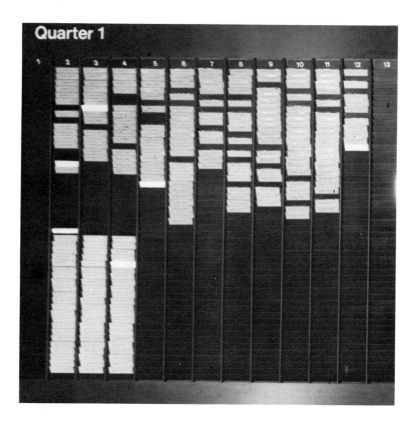

Fig. 24: Planning Board

(iii) *Quarter Plan.* (See Figure 24. All the planning boards are much the same varying only in size and fitting to suit their purpose.) This is a plan divided vertically into thirteen columns, one per week. It may be divided horizontally into three sections – electrical, engineering and deck departments; it contains maintenance planning cards and defect notes.

(iv) *Monthly Maintenance Plan.* All items of monthly maintenance are shown on this plan. It is vertically divided into four columns (one per week) and horizontally into three sections (one per department). Planning is done on a weekly basis, using planning cards on the board and each week one column is transferred to the weekly plan and planned on a daily basis. When these tasks are completed, the appropriate planning cards are returned to the monthly plan.

(v) *Weekly Programme and Work Plan.* Programme :- used to plan and display work to be carried out over one week on a daily basis; it holds maintenance operational (other than watch keeping) Planning Cards and Defect Notes in racks, with smaller racks inside carrying Job Number Cards and Job Supervisor Cards. Work Plan :- shows work force allocation on an hourly basis for the day, with watchkeepers' watches shown by block colouring; transparent 'Cobex' over the work plan allows pencilling in of personnel and job allocation (using job numbers).

(vi) *Mechanics' Rounds Routes.* These specify the areas to be covered on rounds, showing the relevant checks and recordings required for the engineer's log. Normal pressures/temperatures are shown as a guide and an aid to training.

(vii) *Engine Room Servicing Plan.* This is a local planning board showing Planning Cards for items of servicing to be undertaken by watchkeepers on watch. W.I.C.'s are included where applicable.

The operation of this system is best explained by a flow chart (see Figure 25). This firm also offers a fabric maintenance package, which can be incorporated into the p.m. system. It is designed in such a way the inspection routines are used to initiate work. Back-up information is also provided to assist the execution of the work.

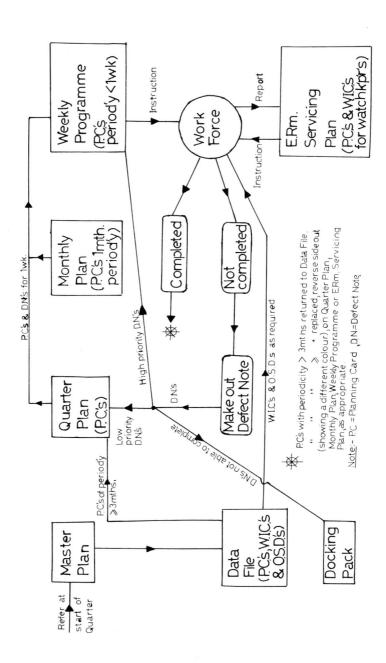

Fig. 25: Planning System (Example 'B')

Example C – Manufacturer. This company sells or rents radio and electronic navigational equipment to a very large number of merchant ship operators. It also provides extensive operating and maintenance services for their equipment on an international scale. These services take the form of shipboard radio officers, who have maintenance duties as well as operating ones, together with agents and depots throughout the world. The company's head office is in the U.K. and most of their expertise is based there.

The company has developed p.m. schedules which, at the time of the investigations, only covered a very limited range of radios and radars. However, a form of p.m. can apply to all the equipment manufactured by the company. A spares system, covering all their equipment, also exists.

There are many different ways in which the shipowner can obtain the equipment, either rented or purchased, with or without sea going operators, and this affects whether or not the shipowner pays an extra charge for the installation and running of the p.m. system, which is carried out by the radio company. It is, however, possible for a shipowner to use the p.m. system while employing his own operators.

The p.m. system described here is basically, but not entirely, a planned inspection (i.e. a condition monitoring) system, based on calendar time, giving an indication of the state of the equipment. Generally, the more serious maintenance and repair work is done by shore personnel. Copies of all maintenance records and reports are retained on board, the originals being forwarded to the nearest company depot to assess the work required. After the work has been completed, the original reports etc. (plus any other relevant documents) are sent to the company's head office for inspection and filing in the ship's own files.

With regard to the p.m. schedules (see Figure 26), each schedule covers one item of equipment. The first section of the schedule explains the contents and how it should be completed, together with tuning and setting-up instructions etc. The second section is concerned with monthly checks. Twelve small charts are provided, one to be used per year. Down the left side of the chart different checks are given a code (1 A, 1

Crusader — Monthly Checks

Transmitter

Select the HF DUMMY LOAD on the Aerial Selector Switch.
Switch on SWA (Mains switch) on the power supplies unit.

1A Check that Power Supplies Lamp LP1 lights.

Set up the Crusader for 8MHz CW operation.

SIDEBAND GENERATOR UNIT

1B Check that Indicator lamps are functioning normally:

FILS	LAMP—LP2
READY	LAMP—LP1
HT	LAMP—LP4
OVERLOAD	LAMP—LP3

FREQUENCY GENERATOR

1C Check that the CRYSTAL OVEN lamp LP1 and the RECEIVER
DRIVE LAMP LP2 are functioning normally.

DRIVE AMPLIFIER AND FINAL STAGE UNITS

Check the following readings on the FEED meter, and record on the chart the
FINAL COLUMN READINGS (FULL POWER).

Meter Switch SWB Position	FSD	SSB2	CW No drive	HF CW (Full Power)
1D V1	25mA	12mA	12mA	12mA
1E V2	25mA	13mA	13mA	13mA
1F V3	100mA	44mA	44mA	44mA
1G V4	100mA	44mA	44mA	44mA
1H V5	250mA	55mA	55–60mA	90mA
1I V5 drive	500mA			160mA
1J FS drive	500mA			230mA
1K FS Cath	500mA	170mA	120mA	480mA
1L FS Fils	20Vrms=500	10Vrms=250	10Vrms=250	10Vrms=250
1M FS HT	5kV	4.2kV	4.2kV	4.0kV

Set Meter Switch SWB to FS CATH

1N Check when operating on Full Power that the correct Drive is obtained
with the RF DRIVE control at about mid position.

Monthly Checks chart

YEAR ....

REF	INITIAL READING	JAN	FEB	MAR	APR	MAY	JUN	JUL	AUG	SEP	OCT	NOV	DEC
1A													
1B													
1C													
1D													
1E													
1F													
1G													
1H													
1I													
1J													
1K													
1L													
1M													
1N													
2A													
2B													
2C													
2D													

Fig. 26: Extracts from PM Schedules

Raymarc 1, 12/16   Monthly Maintenance   (Mechanical/Electrical)

Display

(1) Check the Oldham Coupling in the deflector coil drive system for free rotation by turning it manually.

(2) Check that the Aerial Alignment control pulls in and out freely.

(3) Check that all the Display Push Buttons have positive action.

(4) Check the bearing cursor for smooth operation.

(5) Confirm that all Display controls are fixed securely, and that their respective indicating pointers are aligned.

(6) Clean the bearing cursor face with Perspex Polish, and polish the Plotter glass surfaces.

(7) Check all Display panel illumination, and replace any defective lamps.

Transmitter

(1) Check that the TV plugs for the Sync and Video cables are secure.

(2) Check that the TV plugs fitted to the Pre-IF amplifier are secure, and also ensure that the fixing screw retaining the Pre-IF amplifier is tight.

Raymarc 1, 12/16   Six Monthly Maintenance   (Mechanical)

Inverter

(1) Check that all fuse ratings are correct, and that all fuses are secure within the fuse holders.

(2) Examine the contacts of 'start relay' RLA, and clean if necessary.

Transmitter

(1) Check that all fuse ratings are correct, and that fuses are secure within the fuse holders.

(2) Ensure that there is no dust accumulation around the EHT components, and valve bases.

(3) Check that the valve retainers are correctly fitted.

Display

(1) Clean the scan coil slip rings with 'Brasso'.

(2) Replace the brush assembly if the brushes are well worn down.

(3) Check the operation of all push buttons.

(4) Check that all plugs and sockets are connected firmly.

(5) Check that the 'Oldham Coupling' between the PPI drive motor and gear box has free movement.

(6) Check that all fuse ratings are correct, and that fuses are secure within the fuse holders.

Top and bottom couplings, secured by allen screws requiring 1/20 inch allen key, A/c No. TMS62

End casting supporting PPI drive motor.

Nylon coupling A/c No.CPL66

73

B, 2 A, etc) and the chart is divided into vertical columns, one per month. On separate pages there are detailed, but easy to follow, instructions on how each check should be carried out. Due to the construction of the schedule it is very easy to see which instruction goes with which check on the chart. The chart shows initial readings (entered on installation or after most recent thorough inspection) with which the readings at each check are compared. The radio officer then enters, under the appropriate month, the suitable mark, i.e:

$\sqrt{}$ = satisfactory comparison,
R = satisfactory after readjustment,
F = satisfactory after fault eliminated,
X = fault condition not cleared.

At the end of each year, the completed chart is refiled in the schedule's folder, so that the chart for the following year can be commenced.

The third section deals with monthly and six-monthly electrical and mechanical maintenance (as opposed to just checks). Detailed instructions explain this maintenance. The final section gives a list of spares for the equipment.

The particular benefits of the schedules are intended to be, firstly, that the radio officer benefits by having an early warning of any fault and can refer to past normal readings when a failure does occur, and secondly, that on joining a vessel he can quickly assess the condition of the equipment by referring to the schedules.

The reporting and recording documentation covers all this company's equipment unless, for example, the shipowner purchases the equipment, uses his own operators and does not wish to take advantage of the service. This documentation consists of the following:

(i) *Voyage Maintenance Record* (see Figure 27). This record is vertically divided into columns for weekly checks, monthly routine maintenance and six-monthly routine maintenance. Items of equipment are recorded horizontally across the form. The weekly checks require the radio officer to enter a tick, in the appropriate square, against each piece of equipment to indicate its performance during the preceeding week,

To: (as applicable)   THE MARCONI INTERNATIONAL MARINE CO. LTD.

WHITE COPY — HEAD OFFICE
PINK COPY   — REPORTING DEPOT   **VOYAGE MAINTENANCE RECORD**
BLUE COPY   — SHIP'S FILE

SHEET No.............

Continued on Sheet No. ....

VESSEL ....   CALL LETTERS ....   Names of *Electronics/Radio Officers

Voyage commenced at   .... Date .... No.........

Voyage completed at   .... Date .... No.........

Last Annual Overhaul at   .... Date .... No.........

*delete as necessary

INDIVIDUAL EQUIPMENT	CONDITION	WEEKLY OPERATIONAL CHECKS						** enter date and initial	
		*JULY JAN	AUG FEB	SEPT MAR	OCT APRIL	NOV MAY	DEC JUNE	MONTHLY ROUTINE MAINTENANCE	SIX MONTHLY ROUTINE MAINTENANCE **
		1 2 3 4 5	1 2 3 4 5	1 2 3 4 5	1 2 3 4 5	1 2 3 4 5	1 2 3 4 5	1 2 3 4 5 6	
	Satisfactory / Fair / Unuseable								
	Satisfactory / Fair / Unuseable								
	Satisfactory / Fair / Unuseable								
	Satisfactory / Fair / Unuseable								
	Satisfactory / Fair / Unuseable								
	Satisfactory / Fair / Unuseable								
	Satisfactory / Fair / Unuseable								
	Satisfactory / Fair / Unuseable								
	Satisfactory / Fair / Unuseable								
	Satisfactory / Fair / Unuseable								
	Satisfactory / Fair / Unuseable								
	Satisfactory / Fair / Unuseable								
	Satisfactory / Fair / Unuseable								
	Satisfactory / Fair / Unuseable								
	Satisfactory / Fair / Unuseable								

This is to certify that the operational checks were entered weekly and the Monthly and Six Monthly Maintenance was carried out as laid down in the PLANNED MAINTENANCE SCHEDULE, to the best of my ability.

.... *Electronics/Radio Officer

.... Date

A GEC—MARCONI ELECTRONICS COMPANY

Fig. 27: Voyage Maintenance Record

i.e. satisfactory, fair, and unusable. If the performance is less than satisfactory, the radio officer should investigate and take any necessary action. A Service Report should then be compiled detailing the attention given.

The monthly maintenance columns refer to the completion of the p.m. schedules. As the schedules are completed a tick is entered in the appropriate box in the Voyage Maintenance Record.

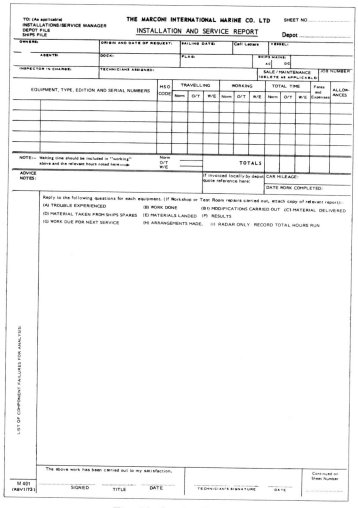

Fig. 28: Service Report

Every six months some specialised maintenance and inspection should be done by the radio officer, such as cleaning, oiling and greasing of mechanical assemblies and checking shipborne spares against lists provided. Details of this work can be found in the p.m. schedules or, with considerably more difficulty, in the instruction manuals. The date of completion of this work, for each piece of equipment, is then entered in the six-monthly column of the Voyage Maintenance Record and initialed by the radio officer. Where possible, he should do this work early in the voyage, so that he can monitor the results of his own maintenance.

(ii) *Service Report* (see Figure 28). This is a form which may be used by either sea or shore staff. A radio officer would only complete it if he had to carry out any work outside the normal maintenance programme. The form indicates what information must be entered, e.g. spares used, modifications carried out. It must state whether or not work is satisfactorily completed and, if not, details of remaining difficulties. The time spent on this work must also be shown. The radio officer may, if he feels it necessary, make a more extensive report of work he has carried out. If overseas agents carry out any work, he should send the relevant Service Report to the company's head office by airmail immediately.

(iii) *Radio Officer's End of Voyage Reporting Form* (see Figure 29). At the end of each voyage, when the radio officer is due to leave the ship, or every three months, this form must be completed. The master's signature is also required and his comments are encouraged, being of interest to, among other people, the company's sales department. The radio officer enters (for all equipment for which he is responsible):

(a) title of equipment;

(b) service contract code for each piece of equipment, (a card on all ships explains this simple one or two letter code which, essentially, indicates who pays for the service);

(c) modification state (from modification label on equipment);

(d) code numbers for performance and reliability (code is explained on form and goes from 1 = excellent to 7 = unusable);

WHITE COPY—HEAD OFFICE		**MARCONI MAR**
PINK COPY —REPORTING DEPOT		
BLUE COPY —SHIP'S COPY		**RADIO OFFICER'S END OF VOYAGE REPOR**

Notes on Compilation

1. Example :
   Crusader TX
   Crusader PU

2. Marconi Service
   Organisation
   Code.

3. Main Unit
   Serial
   Numbers.

4. PDS State.
   Insert last
   number and
   letter crossed
   off relevant
   label
   e.g.—

   X X X 4
   X B C D
   = 3A.

5. Insert appropriate
   Code Symbol to
   describe perform-
   ance & reliability
   throughout
   voyage.
   1. Excellent.
   2. Very Good.
   3. Good.
   4. Fair.
   5. Poor.
   6. Very Poor.
   7. Unuseable.

6. Enter Yes or No
   if attention
   required.
   If Yes describe
   symptoms in
   space on right
   hand side of
   form.

7. Inspector should
   initial following
   inspection.
   Service require-
   ments should be
   briefly indicated
   on right hand
   side of this
   form.

Depot Use Only

Service Bulletin
Checked.

PDS State
Checked and
Updated.

Signed...................

Date.....................

To :

Depot

Arrived From :

Date :

Previous Reporting Form Nr.:
Port :
Date :

Owners :

Destination :

Sailing Date :

Radio Officer :
Name :
Nr.:

(1)

Agents :

Place of last MOT In

Date :

Radio Officer :
Name :
Nr.:

EQUIPMENT

	1	2	3	4	5		6	7	
NAME OF MAIN UNIT	service CODE	SERIAL NUMBER	P.D.S. STATE	CODE		ATTENTION REQD. YES or NO	INSPECTOR'S INITIALS	N
				PERF.	REL.			
Main Transmitter									
									S
Emergency Transmitter									
Accumulators									C
A.K.D.									
R/Telephone									Ti
Main Receiver(s)									A
									P
Emergency Receiver									
V.H.F.									
D/Finder									
Auto Alarm									
Echosounder									
LB (Portable)									

Have all Spares been requisitioned to complete Spares Holding ... ... Yes ☐ No ☐ Ha

Is an up-to-date List of Spares on board ... ... Yes ☐ No ☐ Ha

Has a Spares Location List been compiled ... ... Yes ☐ No ☐ Ae

Are all Official Documents on board and corrected up to date ... ... Yes ☐ No ☐ Is

ATTENTION RECEIVED ABROAD (If any) :—N.B. All Service obtained abroad to be reported immediate

SET	DATE	WHERE	BY WHOM

Master's Comments (if any) :—

Fig. 29: Radio Officer's Reporting Form

NICAL) VESSEL...

	Call Letters :	Radio Certificate valid until :

ltage :		Articles :	Ship's Telephone :
ce :	AC/DC	ON/OFF	Exchange :
:	AC/DC		Nr.:
icer :	(3)	Radio Officer Name : Nr.	(4)

1 9

RADIO OFFICER'S SERVICE REQUIREMENTS :—

3	4	5		6	7
SERIAL NUMBER	P.D S. STATE	CODE		ATTENTION REQD. YES or NO	INSPECTOR'S INITIALS
		PERF.	REL.		

INSPECTOR'S INITIAL INSPECTION REPORT :—

n Checks been carried out during this voyage   ... Yes ☐ No ☐
been carried out as in appropriate handbook   ... Yes ☐ No ☐
rd or on requisition   ...   . Yes ☐ No ☐
on requisition   ...   . Yes ☐ No ☐

material supplied, approximate time and number of technicans.

EPORT .O.	REMARKS

Date.................................

Radio Officer

.... Signed....................................

Form S.299

79

(e) service requirements;

(f) ticks in boxes against a list of administrative duties, e.g. requisitioning of spares;

(g) record of all occasions where a service agent has carried out work on board.

The inspector adds his initials and comments against the report on each piece of equipment.

(iv)*Ship's Service File.* The shipboard file contains copies of maintenance and service reports, i.e. Voyage Maintenance Records, Service Reports (from sea and shore staff), all letters to and from the vessel relating to service, Government survey documents, company documents and technical particulars. Yearly p.m. Schedule Records are retained in their own folder and the radio officer's End Of Voyage Reports are placed in the ship's equipment log book.

The Voyage Maintenance Records, Service Reports and radio officer's End of Voyage Reports are completed in triplicate (using different coloured sheets with carbon paper), one copy being sent to the radio company's head office, one to the next local depot and one copy held on board. If a vessel is away from the U.K. for more than three months, the ship should forward the head office's copies of these reports to the services department at three-monthly intervals.

All reports to the radio company are not automatically sent to the shipping company. However, if the shipping company asks for reports (e.g. wishes to include the electronic equipment within its own p.m. scheme) it is the radio company's policy that the radio officer should comply, confining himself to facts and not giving his personal opinion. He should also send a copy of any such report to the radio company's office.

This company has composed a detailed manual on the operation of its p.m. and spares system, the paperwork involved, and also goes some of the way to explaining good maintenance philosophy. One of these manuals should be available to each of its radio officers at sea.

Extensive and detailed instruction manuals are also provided with all company equipment. These manuals cover operation and maintenance, including fault diagnosis flow charts etc. Even more detailed explanations of checking and maintenance procedures are to be found in the p.m. Schedules, but this, of course, only applies to the limited amount of equipment which these schedules cover.

If a radio officer needs urgent technical advice from the radio company head office he can obtain it via radio telegram or air mail. If he has been following a step-by-step procedure from the company's hand book, a lot of explanation can be avoided by simply quoting the last reference number in the procedure.

Shipboard spares operate on what is basically a minimum or re-order level system. If the number of any spares falls below the level indicated on the spares lists (to be found in the equipment manuals, p.m. Schedules or inside the lid of the spares box), a requisition should be made. The company do however ask that, when possible, the requisitions should be sent in groups. This limits administration and distribution expenses.

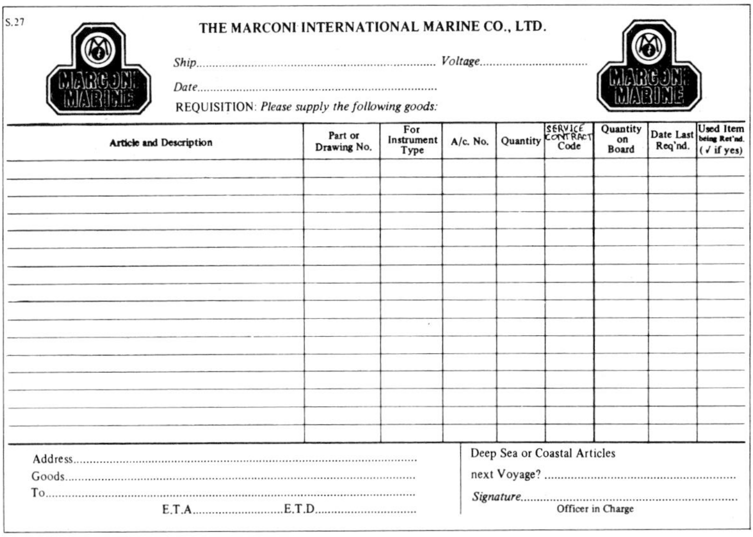

S.27

THE MARCONI INTERNATIONAL MARINE CO., LTD.

Ship.................... *Voltage*....................

Date....................

REQUISITION: *Please supply the following goods:*

Article and Description	Part or Drawing No.	For Instrument Type	A/c. No.	Quantity	SERVICE CONTRACT Code	Quantity on Board	Date Last Req'nd.	Used Item being Ret'nd. (✓ if yes)

Address....................

Goods....................

To....................

E.T.A.................... E.T.D....................

Deep Sea or Coastal Articles

next Voyage? ....

Signature....................

Officer in Charge

Fig. 30: Requisition Form

The company have a standard Requisition Form, shown in Figure 30. (The part or drawing numbers and the account numbers required by this form appear on the spares list). Separate forms should be completed for priority spares and for certain types of service contracts. If spares are to be bought by the shipping company, the radio officer must first obtain authorisation.

Requisitions from ships overseas should be sent to the radio company's supplies department. Ships returning to the U.K.should send their requisitions to their ports of destination. The company strongly emphasise that duplicate requisitions should never be sent, as this could result in double ordering.

The p.m. and spares systems described here are examples of those which could be provided by manufacturers of marine equipment. Of course, in the main, this company also provides an operator/maintainer with their equipment which allows the company to provide extensive documentation with their systems without the fear of adding to the paper work of the shipowners' personnel.

We can make two observations about this company. Firstly, there are separate p.m. schedules for each item of equipment. This differs from most p.m. scheduling systems where all the equipment considered is covered under one schedule. The disadvantage of having separate schedules for different items of equipment is that unless the schedules are phased suitably with each other the total workload will not spread evenly, leading to work back-logs, disillusionment, lack of commitment etc. Overall scheduling can only be achieved, for ship's radio and electronic equipment, by taking account of that particular ship's combination of equipment. This would involve considerably more work for the radio company in setting up schedules. Alternatively, the shipping company could undertake this task, using the radio company's individual equipment schedules.

Secondly, the company seems to firmly believe in formal reporting methods, using standardised forms. When one considers the number of ships with which the company is dealing, the many different types of equipment it supplies and the complexity of this equipment, such methods of reporting seem inevitable. Also the various report forms provide a type of maintenance and inspection schedule which, to a very limited extent, fulfils the roles of all the normal p.m. system components.

Let us now consider a less formal system, where the planning and instruction of the work is very largely left to the shipboard personnel.

Example D – Shipping Company. This company manages about fifty ships on world-wide voyages. The engineering superintendents cover all maintenance on ships (other than furnishings) and the chief engineers and chief officers are immediately responsible to them. The chief engineer is ultimately responsible for all maintenance on board, but the chief officer controls deck cleanliness, painting and cargo equipment. Should repair work arise in this area, however, the chief engineer would control it.

The crews are mainly British with Chinese or West Indians on some vessels. Some crews are general purpose. The ships drydock approximately every eighteen months.

Let us first consider engine room and machinery maintenance. Lloyds surveys are shown on a five-year chart. As surveys are completed they are inked in on the chart. Chief engineers empowered by Lloyds can carry out certain minor surveys. Details of maintenance work other than surveys are enclosed in a shipboard file for the chief engineer to refer to. This gives instructions on how to carry out work, with reference to manufacturers' manuals carried on board, where necessary. It also gives the periodicities of the jobs to be carried out (on a running hours basis for all main machinery), and acts as a basic policy statement. No formalised planning is given however, and it is up to the chief engineer to plan the work in whatever way he thinks best. Normally he would recruit the help of the 2nd Engineer to help him with this task, and therefore the effectiveness of the planning depends on the skill, training and experience of these two in work planning.

The chief engineer writes a report of work done each voyage – one copy being kept as a record on board, the other

```
                                                              Form D11


                          MAINTENANCE RECORD

     MV/SS _____

     For Voyage Nos._____

     Arriving at _____  On _____

     Date of last record submitted _____


                                      _____ Chief Officer

                                      _____ Master


     Instructions to Chief Officers

          Reports should detail all maintenance work done since the previous report, including that
     undertaken by other Departments. Reference to routine washing, greasing and similar work should
     be omitted. Work undertaken by shore contractors should be included but marked (S/C).

          Reports should be submitted at the end of each voyage or as otherwise instructed. A running
     copy is to be maintained on board available for inspection at all times.

          Following completion, all pages of the report are to be secured by one staple in the top left
     hand corner.
```

(fig. 31)

sent to head office. Should any breakdown work occur during the voyage, he must write a report on this (in letter form) for head office. He must also complete a standard voyage report showing fuel consumption, running hours, etc. for head office. No coding system is used for these reports, but everything identified by its name.

The deck maintenance system is very basic, but the company argue that this is all that is possible since their vessels' runs are such that little time is left for maintenance work and it would be impossible for their crews to conform to any pre-arranged maintenance schedule. The only formalised documentation that head office imposes on the ships are Maintenance Records, which must be completed by the chief officer once per voyage. They do, in fact, assume the role of Report and Shipboard Record, since one copy is sent to head office, the other retained on board. They also, to a very limited extent, act as a Master Plan spanning one voyage since, because of their format, they indicate broadly what

MAINTENANCE RECORD—exterior (cont)   Page 4

Area	Date last painted	Work done since last report	Supts. comments
Winches			
Windlass/ Docking winches			
Funnel			
Swimming pool			
Lifeboats, exterior No.			
Lifeboats, interior No.			
Davits, winches			

LIFEBOAT GEAR

S.E. Cert expires
Liferaft survey due

Boat No.	Stores Checked	Falls Renewed	Falls Ended	Gripes Renewed	Spans Renewed		Expiry date
						Distress rockets	
						Lifeboat outfits	
						Smoke floats	
						Linethrow rockets	
						Linethrow cartridges	

GANGWAY FALLS		Falls Renewed	Falls Ended	PILOT HOIST	Wires Renewed	Wires Ended
Starboard						
Port						

STORES CRANE		Last overhaul	Wires Renewed	ENGINE ROOM CRANE	Last overhaul	Wires Renewed

Fig. 31: Maintenance Record Extract

work must be considered. Figure 31 shows an excerpt from this record. It is a fairly good example of a standardised reporting/recording form, being reasonably simple and yet making it clear what information is required.

It is largely left to the discretion of the chief officer exactly what jobs should be tackled and to what depth, depending on need, time available, manpower, etc. Thus, like the chief and 2nd engineer, the effectiveness of the maintenance planning depends on the chief officer, i.e. his skill, training and experience. Because the standard of maintenance, both in the engine room and on deck, depends to such a large extent upon the ability of the responsible officers, the company must ensure, by training and career planning, that they possess such ability.

It is worth noting that in this company (as in many) much of the navigational and radio equipment is rented, and maintenance on this equipment is carried out by the manufacturers, and radio operators who are employees of the manufacturers. However, brief reports on this equipment are included in the company voyage reports to head office (e.g. 'Satisfactory' and 'Repair work still to be done').

4.3   *Back-up Information*

If a good quality of maintenance work on board is to be expected then adequate back-up information must be supplied to the ship. Job Specifications, already discussed at length in Chapter 2, although extremely useful for supplying 'on the spot' information for the man doing the job, are not sufficient in themselves. The seafarer needs more detailed information to fall back on, when required. Some manufacturers' manuals are quite reasonable in fulfilling this need, especially those concerning established 'marinised' equipment, but many others can vary from being little more than a sales leaflet to somewhat of an 'overkill' talking over the heads of most on board. There are, then, several advantages of producing tailor-made manuals for a vessel. The main advantage is that all of a ship's equipment may be covered uniformly, rather than some in depth and some hardly at all, thus making it much easier for the seafarer to obtain the information he seeks. Also, interfaces between different pieces of equipment and different systems may be covered, whereas if relying solely on manufacturers' manuals they very often would not be.

A similar argument applies to spares manuals. As stated in Chapter 3, a Spares Policy Statement may well be incorporated into a spares manual, and thus the manual can provide a uniform coverage of all the information on spares that those on board may need – without recourse to manufacturers' manuals, chasing manufacturers' codes for ordering, etc...

Some shipping companies have attempted the task of composing these manuals (for maintenance and spares) themselves, but most have gone to consultancy firms who, in the main, do a good job in this respect.

Another way of providing back-up information on certain maintenance tasks, as well as providing an on-board training facility, is the placing of audio visual systems aboard, such as closed-circuit television tapes, films or the system shown in Example F. Shown here are three good examples of attempts to provide different types of shipboard back-up information.

Example E – Consultancy Firm's Technical Manuals Service. The stated purpose of this service is to provide information to the crew as an aid to the correct and safe operation of plant and machinery, crew training and efficient maintenance and repair. The service ranges from organisation and 'customisation' of existing information to the creation of new system operating and maintenance manuals for a specific vessel. It may be broken down into the following components:

(i) *Technical Data Organisation Service.* This service provides the ship and head office with a package of technical information (broken down into a system index), customised for each ship. It is reduced to microfiche (24× reduction) and supplied with the appropriate viewing and reproduction equipment. To accomplish this, information must be accumulated and indexed, manuals edited and customised, and then the information filmed. This service is usually confined to spares information but need not necessarily be so.

(ii) *Unit Location Diagrams* (see Figure 32). An on-board survey is necessary to gather the information to compile these diagrams. They include detailed illustrations of units and show the locations of items such as key-valves etc. They are indexed in the standard way and produced on durable stock in loose-leaf binders.

(iii) *Operating and Maintenance Manuals.* These provide system and machine operating instructions, which are not of direct interest here. However, they may also include trouble-shooting guides, to provide rapid fault identification at systems level, and detailed, illustrated, servicing instructions (see Figure 33) and repairs procedures for items which require this particularly detailed treatment, e.g. cranes. These manuals are cross-indexed to the unit location diagrams.

(iv) *Check Lists* (see Figure 34). These lists may be designed for systems or individual units. They are job specifications of operational work, ensuring that operational procedures are not overlooked, especially at times of high activity. They are not directly related to maintenance but could prevent damage occurring requiring subsequent maintenance.

(It should be noted that this firm can also provide fully integrated p.m. and spares control systems, which can be computer linked, providing a management data analysis service).

Example F – Audio Visual Instruction System. This system is called M.A.V.I.S. (Marine Audio Visual Instructional Systems) and their units and programmes are to be found on many ships at the present time. Various types of displays are available; small or large screen self-contained units (Figure 35 shows a small screen type), a projector which can be used with any standard screen, or a unit which has its own screen and can also project.

The programmes themselves consist of colour stills from a 16 mm film strip running in synchronisation with a commentary on an audio magnetic tape. Both film strip and tape are enclosed in a cartridge (see Figure 36) which is simply slotted into the display unit. The programme may be stopped

88

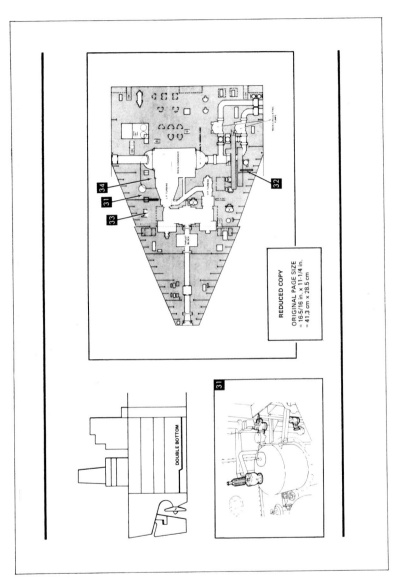

Fig. 32: Unit Location Diagram

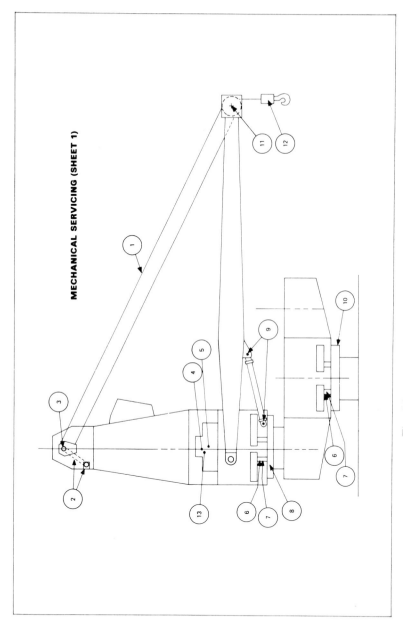

MECHANICAL SERVICING (SHEET 1)

Fig. 33: Mechanical Servicing Sheet Extract

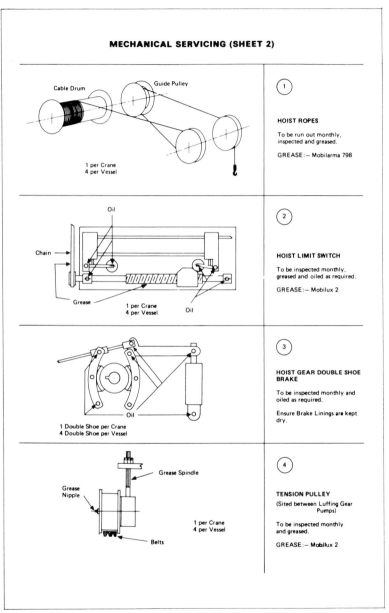

MECHANICAL SERVICING (SHEET 2)

①

Cable Drum — Guide Pulley

HOIST ROPES

To be run out monthly, inspected and greased.

GREASE:— Mobilarma 798

1 per Crane
4 per Vessel

②

Oil

Chain

HOIST LIMIT SWITCH

To be inspected monthly, greased and oiled as required.

GREASE:— Mobilux 2

Grease

1 per Crane
4 per Vessel

Oil

③

HOIST GEAR DOUBLE SHOE BRAKE

To be inspected monthly and oiled as required.

Ensure Brake Linings are kept dry.

Oil

1 Double Shoe per Crane
4 Double Shoe per Vessel

④

Grease Spindle

Grease Nipple

TENSION PULLEY

(Sited between Luffing Gear Pumps)

To be inspected monthly and greased.

GREASE:— Mobilux 2

1 per Crane
4 per Vessel

Belts

(fig. 33)

OILCRAFT			MACHINERY CHECK OFF LIST	

PROCEDURE	No. 11	TITLE PREPARE AND OPERATE TURBO ALTERNATOR		

RELATED INSTRUCTIONS (Note: The numbers listed in the "step" column below correspond to the numbered steps within the related instructions) **PREPARE AND OPERATE TURBO ALTERNATOR**

CHECK LISTS PREVIOUSLY COMPLETED (Note: These check lists must be completed before proceeding with this check list)

5. PREPARE L.P. AND MAINTAINED EXHAUST SYSTEMS

STEP	INSTRUCTION/CHECK	TICK COMPLETE	REMARKS
1.	Check supply of salt water		
2.	Check valve list		
3.	Check valve list		
4.	Check LO sump level		
5.	Start auxiliary LO pump		
6.	Check mobility of main stop valve		
7.	Check mobility of throttle valve		
8.	Check back pressure system		
9.	Check valve list		
10.	Start gland condenser fan		
11.	Set hand trip		
12.	Reset master trip valve		
13.	Set speed governor		
14.	Open boiler valves		
15.	Check drain trap		
16.	Open main steam valve		
17.	Open main stop valve		
18.	Close main stop drain		
19.	Partially open exhaust valve, close exhaust drain		
20.	Fully open exhaust valve		
21.	Continue to open main stop valve until turbine starts		
22.	Check for undue noise, accelerate turbine		
23.	Fully open main stop		
24.	Check auxiliary LO pump		
25.	Test overspeed trip		
26.	Close main stop valve		
27.	Allow turbine speed to fall		
28.	Reset master trip		
29.	Restart turbine		
30.	Fully open main stop valve		

CERTIFIED SATISFACTORILY COMPLETED SUBJECT TO COMMENTS AS STATED: .... Ch. Eng.

Fig. 34: Check List

Fig. 35: M.A.V.I.S. Courier 16

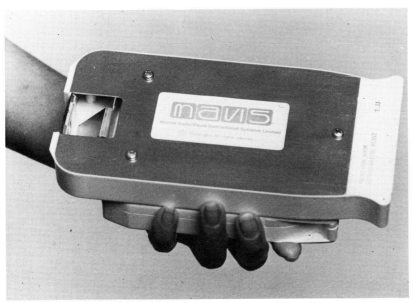

Fig. 36: M.A.V.I.S. Programme Cartridge

93

at any point, so that a particular diagram or picture can be studied as long as is required. A selection of programmes and a display unit can be compactly stowed away in a case.

The programmes, which can only be produced by M.A.V.I.S. themselves, cover a wide range of subjects but many of them concern maintenance. Some of these programmes consist of 'blow by blow' instructions for, say, a particular item of machinery, providing detailed operational and maintenance back-up information, as well as training, on that item. Others are of a more general nature covering, for example, painting or welding techniques and are intended purely for training purposes. The smaller units, although requiring mains power, are light and robust and may often be transported to the sight of the equipment to which they refer.

M.A.V.I.S. claim that they can produce programmes at a cost of around one tenth of that of a normal industrial training film.

Example G – Shipping Company's Spares Manuals. This company has a large world-wide tanker operation, often to ports where maintenance and spares facilities are very limited, thus the reliability of these ships must be high. The p.m. and spares systems of this company are therefore relatively advanced. The spares system is based on re-order and maximum stock levels, as described in Chapter 3. A company spares ordering code is also incorporated, thus simplifying ordering by the ship and gaining the economic advantages (bulk ordering etc.) that the use of such a code offers.

On each ship there is a composite spare gear manual which covers all machinery parts and replacement equipment for that ship. Figure 37 shows an excerpt from such a manual, covering a centrifugal pump. The format is as follows:

(i) *Title page* (Figure 37(a)); showing name of unit, company spares ordering code of whole unit, manufacturer, type and size, drawing numbers, with serial numbers and names of ships where fitted in conjunction with the respective location codes (Function – System – Unit, shown as F.S. Unit).

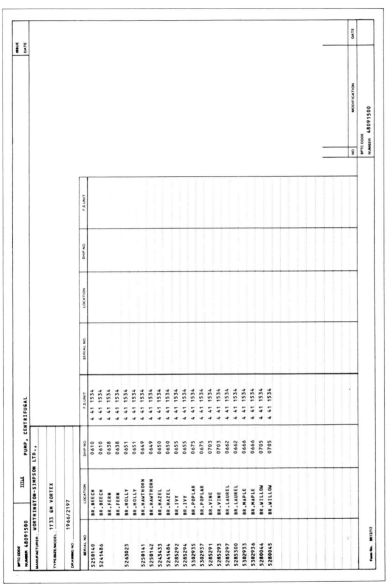

Fig. 37(a): Extract from Spares Manual (Example 'G')

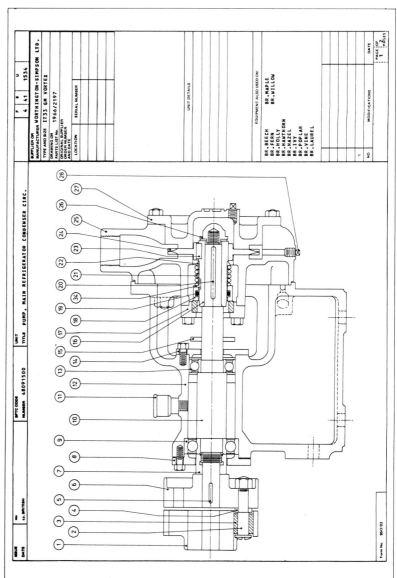

Fig. 37(b)

DIAGRAM REF.	BPTC CODE NUMBER	MAKERS PTO/MOD CODE NUMBER	ITEM DESCRIPTION	UNIT QUANTITY	NUMBER FITTED TO ONE UNIT	USED ON	REMARKS	REORDER LEVEL	MAXIMUM	IN WAREHOUSE
10	48091500	1966/2197	PUMP, COMPLETE	NOS	1					
	48091502	S1061/29	SHAFT	NOS	1			0	1	Y
24	48091503	S1302/7	WHEEL, PUMP	NOS	1			0	1	Y
23	48091504	1/4IN.SQ.X 11/16IN.LG.	FEATHER, PUMP WHEEL	NOS	1	48091503		0	1	Y
16	48091505	S1062/30	SLEEVE, PUMP WHEEL	NOS	1	48091503		0	1	Y
20	48091506	3/16IN.SQ.X 2.9/32IN.LG.	FEATHER, PUMP WHEEL SLEEVE	NOS	1	48091505		0	1	Y
17	48091507	S1188/62	SEAL COVER & FACE	NOS	1			0	1	Y
18	48091508	S1189/33	RING, ROTARY	NOS	1			0	1	Y
19	48091509	S989/20	'O' RING, ROTARY RING	NOS	1			0	1	Y
21	48091510	S1011/40	SPRING	NOS	1			0	1	Y
22	48091511	S1191/23	SEAT, SPRING	NOS	1	48091505		0	1	Y
26	48091512	S1065/1	NUT, PUMP WHEEL SLEEVE	NOS	1			0	1	Y
26	48091513	S997/18	WASHER, FIBRE	NOS	1			0	0	Y
27	48091514	S1301/16	COVER, PUMP	NOS	1					Y
15	48091515	S1067/1	THROWER, WATER	NOS	1			0	1	Y
9	(530596000)	S184/825	BEARING, BALL, D.E.	NOS	1		RHP 6305	0	1	Y
13	(530496000)	S184/A25	BEARING, BALL, P.E.	NOS	1		RHP 6205	0	0	Y
7	48091516	S926/1	LOCKNUT, BEARING	NOS	1					Y
8	48091517	S298/3	COVER, D.E. BEARING	NOS	1					Y
11	48091518	S993/1	LUBRICATOR, STAUFFER	NOS	1					Y
14	48091519	S1060/4	COVER, P.E. BEARING	NOS	1					Y
6	48091520	S188/18	COUPLING, PUMP HALF	NOS	1					Y
1	48091521	K16A	COUPLING, MOTOR HALF	NOS	4			2	4	Y
2	48091522	K19A	PIN C/W NUT, COUPLING	NOS	4			2	4	Y
4	48091523	S209/1	COLLAR, COUPLING PIN	NOS	4					Y
3	48091524	K17	BUSH, COUPLING PIN	NOS	4			0	1	Y
5	48091525	3/16IN.SQ.X 15/16IN.LG.	FEATHER, COUPLING	NOS	1					Y
25	48091526	S1300/16	CASING, PUMP	NOS	1			0	1	Y
34	48091527	S1498/1	KEY, SEAL	NOS	1					Y

BPTC CODE NUMBER 48091500

Form No. 9612/05 (11/78)

PAGE 2 OF 2 PAGES

Fig. 37(c)

(ii) *Drawing page(s)* (Figure 37(b)); showing the components of the unit detailed on the breakdown page(s), either in the form of a section drawing or as an index.

(iii) *Breakdown page(s)* (Figure 37(c)); identifying each component or item by reference to the drawing page, a worded description, company spares ordering code and manufacturer's part number. It also shows, for each item, recommended re-order and maximum stock levels and whether the item is stocked in the company warehouse (indicated by a "Y").

The prime purposes of the manual are to provide a shipboard spares policy statement, to identify each item using the company spares ordering code and to present clear, uniform information to shipboard personnel for ordering and recording purposes. Initially the manuals, which must be updated as necessary, were issued on A3 size paper, but this has now been superceded by the use of microfiche.

Chapter 5
Relevant Management Principles

5.1 *Control Systems*

Any maintenance management system exists to control the maintenance operation. It is, therefore, a type of control system and a brief study of the properties of control systems should help at this point.

A system must have an input and an output. There are basically two types of system (see Figure 38):

(i) An *open*, or *direct system* where input is not dependent on output.

(ii) A *closed system*, where some form of link exists so that input varies with output. This link is known as *'feedback'* and its purpose (so far as we are concerned here) is to measure the output and then modify the input until the desired output is obtained. In other words, a control cycle has been formed.

We are interested in the latter system, since maintenance management is, or should be, a control cycle. The feedback loop in this control cycle usually has its own input (i.e. measurement of output of main system) and output (control of input of main system). In other words, it becomes a system in itself, i.e. a *control system*. It may have its own feedback loop, or possibly other inputs which may influence its control, thus becoming quite a complex system. Very often, when studying a control system we find a superior system governing or affecting it and we must also consider this.

To clarify the elements of a control system, they are fundamentally as follows (see Figure 39):

(i) Measurement of the output of the system being controlled.

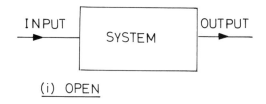

(i) OPEN

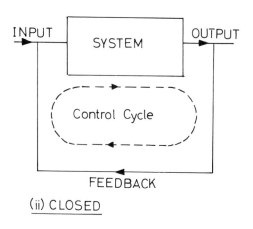

FEEDBACK

(ii) CLOSED

Fig. 38: Systems

(ii) Feedback, i.e. interpretation of measurement information into new input or control parameters.

(iii) A standard, or optimum, possibly set by a superior
system, which the controller needs to compare the measurement information with in order to formulate the new
parameters.

(iv) The operation of control, i.e. applying the new parameters to the system.

But what about the actual control itself? This can be
divided into two sorts. Firstly, there is a type of control which
endeavours to retain stability of a system's operation, or
homeostasis – a biological term meaning an automatic prin-
ciple which maintains stability, e.g. body temperature is controlled by sweating when temperature is too hot and shivering
when too cold. Secondly, control may be of the *innovation*

100

type. In other words it is intended to bring about a change in the system; e.g. modification of a car engine by, say, changing from a single carburettor to twin carburettors if performance requires improvement. Usually, the control of a system is a balance of these two different types.

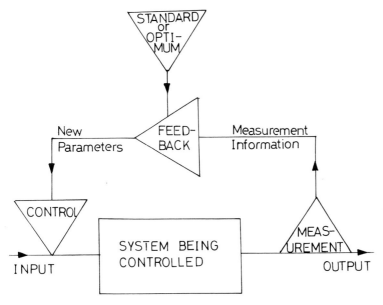

Fig. 39: Control System

There are two types of source or seat of control – *intrinsic* i.e. built into the system being considered and hence operating continuously while the system is functioning, or *extrinsic*, i.e. external to the system being considered and hence not necessarily continuously operational. A control system which is inseparable from the system it controls is therefore intrinsic to it, whereas a control system which could be disconnected or is a spasmodic outside influence would be seen as extrinsic. Many control systems are neither, in the purest sense, but tend towards one or the other. It is also fair to say that where systems have both homeostasis and innovative control, the homeostasis control is usually intrinsic while the innovative is extrinsic.

Let us then apply this theory to shipboard maintenance management. Figure 40 shows the most common acceptable cycle that is likely to exist (although it is difficult to generalise) incorporating the basic p.m. components as described in Chapter 2. In fact, two cycles exist, labelled "X" and "Y". "X" takes place within the ship, controlling the maintenance operation within the plan and the normal capabilities of shipboard personnel. It could be considered as intrinsic homeostasis control. "Y" is a more long-term, or over-view, control cycle, probably existing between the ship and the maintenance department ashore. Its feedback would mainly lead to extrinsic innovation control, altering the Policy Statement and the Master Plan.

5.2 *Communications*

Many management problems are, at least in part, ones of communication. "A" was misunderstood by "B"; "X" omitted to pass the information on to "Y"; "Z" overlooked an important instruction contained in his standing orders, etc. The list is endless. So what exactly do we mean by communications? Basically what is meant is the transmission and reception of information, however, prior to transmission the information must be collected and after reception, acted upon. Information storage may also be included in the process. In the light of all this, 'the handling of information' might be a broader understanding of the term.

Communications, in the widest sense, is an important aspect of maintenance management. This is particularly true of shipboard maintenance management, because of the degree of isolation of ships. Job specifications, reporting, ordering, recording, manuals, plans, verbal discussion, debriefing, etc. are all forms of communication and are covered specifically elsewhere in the book, where various principles of communications are applied to them. However, it is worth discussing the relevant principles and theories of communications on their own here, to clarify some statements in other sections, the full significance of which may not have been seen. It is hoped that this will enable the reader to apply these

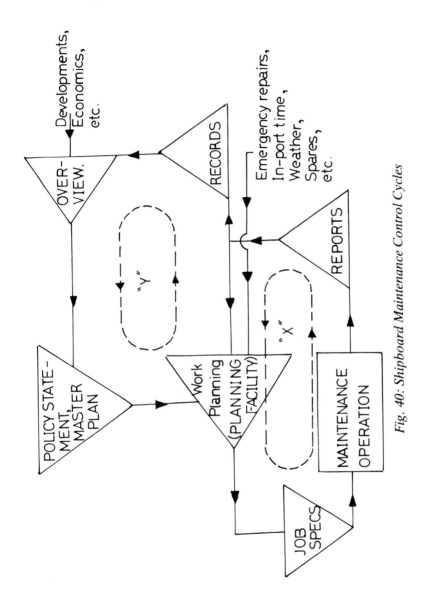

Fig. 40: Shipboard Maintenance Control Cycles

103

principles and theories to communication problems, at least within the context of maintenance management, which he may be confronted with.

Information Collection. When information is being extracted from a system, the system should not be hampered. For example data collection (either reporting or condition data automatically collected) should not detract from the efficiency and working time of either the maintenance personnel or the equipment aboard ship.

Overlaps of data collected should be avoided. This is invariably caused by a lack of integration; e.g. the same data being collected by two departments or by two systems, say a spares system and a p.m. system.

The least time is consumed when 'exception' data only is reported ('by exception' reporting), but this can only be done when a standard (i.e. what is exceptional and what is not) has been established.

Finally, only useful data should be collected, bearing the system's objectives in mind; e.g. there is no point in a report form asking for excessive information on a routine maintenance task when the information will never be analysed and perhaps not even recorded.

Information Transmission and Reception. Once data is collected it must be translated into some language or code and transmitted via some channel. When received it may then have to be translated again, or decoded, and interpreted into a specific action by the receiver. This action could ideally be that intended by the transmitter, if the transmitted information was in the form of an instruction. Alternatively, it could be at the discretion of the receiver after comparing the received information from some other source, such as a standard or an optimum condition (as mentioned in previous section) or his own knowledge and experience. However, during this process of transmission and reception, noise (i.e. irrelevant information) and distortion (of relevant information) may be introduced. Figure 41 illustrates this. A consideration of standardised report forms helps to illustrate these two unwanted elements of communication. If standardised reports are not used, but rather the reporter simply has to write a 'letter' type of report, then almost certainly he will include some amount of 'noise', which head office has no use for. If, on the other hand, a report form is too rigid in its construction, the reporter may not be able to express himself satisfactorily and the report may become distorted. This, in fact, could be regarded as a case of distortion owing to the quantity and type of information being outside the capacity of the channel (i.e. the report form).

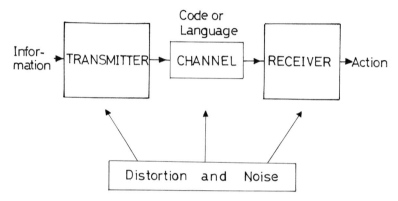

Fig. 41: Information Transmission and Reception

Communication may be one-way, e.g. a manufacturer imparting maintenance information to the maintainers via a manual, or two-way, e.g. a ship's officer discussing the day's maintenance work with his work force. Two-way communication, of course, is usually easier because distortion and noise are more readily eliminated. A lot of care must be taken with one-way communication if it is to be effective. Possible distortion, such as ambiguity of statements or codes, and the ingress of noise, at every stage of the communication process, should be keenly guarded against.

The storage and retrieval of information, e.g. the use of records, can also be looked upon as a communication process. The storage or recording process is the transmitter-to-channel interface, the information being translated into some form, often a code, suitable for storage and future retrieval. The retrieval of information, either in raw or analysed form, is the channel-to-receiver interface. We can, therefore, apply the same basic communication principles to information storage and retrieval as we would to other forms of communication, particularly those relating to distortion and noise. For example any information which is recorded in, say, head office's maintenance records and which will never be used, may be regarded as noise.

Certain points regarding information, and transmission and reception, are raised under 'Information Theory' rather than here, since they come directly from that theory.

Human Factors. Human beings play a large part in the forms of communication which we are considering here. They are the 'transmitters' and 'receivers' (except in some cases where computers can be used) and therefore are absolutely vital in the communication process. This being so, the designers, instigators and participants of a communication system must always bear in mind the feelings, capabilities and reactions of others involved in the system. Background, training and experience of a person all contribute to his 'conceptual framework' and this framework will, together with his present condition, environment, etc., determine how he will report, interpret and act upon any information which he may receive.

The accuracy of reported data can be very much dependent on the reporter. Is it fact, opinion or hearsay? Take, for example, a breakdown report. The reporter might, because of his own defensive mechanism, give a false cause because he feels that otherwise the blame, or some of it, may reflect on him. The reporting system should be aimed at minimising this where possible and, where opinion rather than fact is given, it should be able to identify it as such.

The language, or code, of a communication system must also be completely understandable to everybody concerned, i.e. it must be a common language. This may seem obvious but how often have we all been confronted, at some time or other, with technical jargon, or perhaps a manufacturer's code, which we are obviously expected to understand but in fact have not an inkling as to its meaning.

Finally, when introducing or changing a communication or information system, conflict should be avoided by keeping everyone involved informed on the basic questions 'Why?' and 'How?'. To explain how the system works is, perhaps, obvious – although even this is often ignored. But explaining why the system is necessary is equally important, if not more so. Unless this is done, the motivation and commitment will be lacking. Human nature being what it is, to do something well we need to justify our actions, i.e. we need to realise that it is a good idea. Also, very often if we know why a particular task is necessary, or what the objective of the task is, we are better able to complete it in the required way, thus making the answer to the question 'How?' more obvious.

Information Theory. In its raw form, this theory puts forward a mathematical technique to enable the designer of an information or communication system to minimise the effects of distortion and noise upon his system. However, information theory leads to several important and significant conclusions regarding communications, which are stated here in general, rather than mathematical, terms.

The theory says that the more surprising the event reported, the greater the information gained. This can be directly applied to 'by exception' reporting. It indicates that this is the most efficient way to report, once the required norm is established; e.g. once a p.m. system has become established and fairly stable, it is sensible only to generate reports to head office when the plan has not been complied with. However, it must be said that in the early stages of establishment of a p.m. system it is necessary to report more fully, so that a data bank of information can be built up on the equipment and maintenance tasks. Also the plan can then be closely monitored, and steered more quickly towards the optimum, which then becomes the 'norm'.

According to the theory, any information received can be regarded as being reduced by the amount of prior information available to the recipient, i.e. there is very little point in communicating to somebody what he already knows. Although a seemingly obvious statement, this is an extremely easy mistake to make. Would-be recipients of information can often unknowingly ask for information to which they already have easy access.

What determines the real amount of useful information received in a system is the degree of uncertainty of this information; e.g. could a message be one of two possible statements, or one of a hundred possible statements? If it could be one of a hundred then its degree of uncertainty is much higher, and it contains more information. Imagine someone inviting you to choose a card from a pack of playing cards, and then you describing to that person the card which you hold. If you had a choice of only two possible statements you would probably say whether it was red or black. If you had a choice of fifty-two statements you could say exactly which card it was, thus imparting a lot more information. This degree of uncertainty of information, i.e. its real information content, is measured in terms of 'entropy' (a term borrowed from thermodynamics) within the information theory. For example we may say that spares indents on pieces of equipment with random failure rates will have a higher entropy than spares indents on pieces of equipment with predictable failure rates.

One conclusion drawn from the theory, which is perhaps particularly relevant to codes, is that any change in a communication or information system which tends to equalise the probabilities of occurrence of the various symbols, has the effect of increasing the information content of each statement. This basically leads to simple systems, never using two symbols when one will do; e.g. if the maximum number of digits in a code is to be five, for that code to contain the maximum amount of information each digit must be equally informative.

Essentially, information theory implies that transmitted information must be clear and transmitted in the most effective way while keeping noise to a minimum. A successful communications system is one where there is little difference between the information sent and received. Shannon and Weaver, developers of information theory, recommend that one should ask three questions of any communication system:

(i) How accurately can information be transmitted?

(ii) How accurately does the transmitted information convey the intended meaning?

(iii) How effectively does the received meaning influence the conduct of the recipient in the way desired?

Coding Systems. A coding system can, if properly conceived and used, greatly improve the efficiency of information transmission, reception, storage and retrieval. It can be used (as mentioned in previous chapters) to very good effect in p.m. and spares systems, indentifying maintenance tasks and equipment components. When a code is being conceived, the following points should be considered:

(i) It should be capable of being altered and added to.

(ii) The transmitted code should not contain information which is already known to the receiver or which the receiver has easier access to than the sender.

(iii) It should contain the minimum number of symbols, all with as near equal probabilities of occurrence as possible, thus avoiding unnecessary complexity.

(iv) Any sources of ambiguity should be eliminated.

(v) The more mathematical implications of information theory (other than those mentioned here) should be considered, and applied where practicable.

(vi) The code should, as far as possible, be logical (for cross-checking, etc.).

(vii) The limitations of the channel or store, through or into which the code must be transmitted or stored, must be realised.

(viii) It should, if possible, easily show up coding errors.

To summarise, the code should have a high entropy, with irrelevant information and causes of distortion minimised, and should be as quick and easy to use as possible. Finally, it must be emphasised that everyone involved must always have sufficient means of efficiently coding and decoding any code which they are expected to use, and that this code must be easily identifiable, and not confused with other codes.

5.3   *Decision Making*

A decision is a choice from a set of alternatives. The choice is made with the aim of achieving a goal, which may be a single objective or a set of objectives. If the latter is the case, then these objectives will probably have to be ranked in some sort of priority if the most appropriate decision is to be made. One must also bear in mind that the objectives may alter with the passage of time and changing situations. This can mean the decision having to be changed before the goal is reached, or the decision making process having to be repeated at a later date to achieve the new, modified goal.

Let us examine the ideal decision making process (see Figure 42). It starts with the recognition of a need for a decision to be made. If planning and forecasting are being carried out, this, hopefully, will occur before a crisis situation is reached in most cases. Next there should follow an exploration to bring to light and clarify the objectives, the relevant information and the real constraints. This step is critical. Often, one must not only dig, but know where to dig. It is necessary to distinguish relevant from irrelevant, real from imaginary, and quantify wherever possible. A valid maxim is that *no decision is better than the information upon which it is based.*

The results of the exploration permit the generation of a set of alternatives which may be evaluated. Individual alternatives may be subject to specific constraints. The alternative chosen should be the one which satisfies the objectives best while staying within its specific constraints. It should be stressed here that the natural capability, experience and knowledge of the decision-maker, as well as the facilities available to him, are adequate for him to make an effective decision at the level at which he is operating.

Thus the decision is made and, hopefully, the goal achieved. However, it is important that there should be some kind of feedback on the effectiveness of the decision, i.e. what actually happened should be compared with what the decision-maker thought would happen. The purpose of this feedback is partly to complete the control cycle (see 5.1),

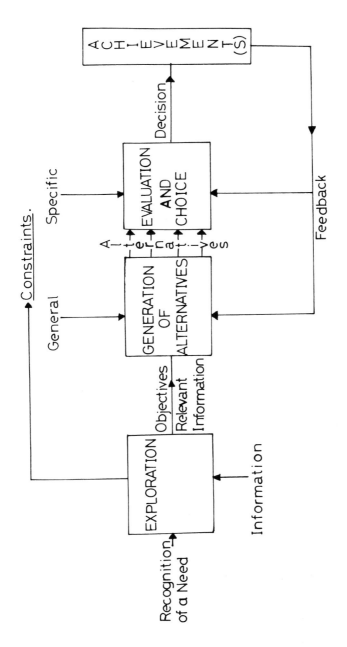

Fig. 42: Decision Making Process

partly to improve the decision making process by assessing its 'efficiency', and partly to study the response of others to your decision (e.g. does it motivate them?) – if the response is not satisfactory one must then try to find out why and put this right.

To illustrate this process, take the simple example of when to paint the deck of, say, a U.K. to Middle East ship.

Recognition of need: Inspection finds deck in poor condition.

Exploration: Man hours required, paint required (is it in stock?), information from company or paint manufacturers on procedures, etc., time (at sea) necessary for job, possible weather, etc.

Objectives: To paint before corrosion gets serious, before deck becomes unsafe and before appearance falls below company's standard.

General constraints: Time at sea is the only time suitable to do the job, weather must be dry, other crew activities, paint characteristics, painting methods.

Alternatives: Complete job (a) last week of outward passage or (b) first week of homeward passage.

Specific constraints: For (a), paint will not have time to fully harden before first port is reached and cargo work starts; for (b) weather – monsoon may start early or ship may be behind schedule.

Evaluation: If (a) adopted, new paint will certainly be ruined; if (b) adopted, unless the ship is very unlucky, dry weather should continue long enough for painting to be completed.

Decision: Alternative (b).

Feedback: Response of the crew, inspection of similar vessel which chose alternative (a), inspection of own ship's deck on the following voyage.

There are two different types, or more precisely levels, of decisions, 'programmed' and 'non-programmed'. Programmed or routine decisions are ones which are made from a completely defined set of rules, predetermined by a system. Such decisions could come within the homeostasis control of a system; e.g. deciding on the spares to order when the maximum, re-order and present stock levels are all defined by the spares stock control system. Non-programmed decisions are unique. The relevant information and constraints are often not well defined or so easily available and a higher degree of uncertainty often exists. They could be planning decisions or decisions which may come within the innovative control of a system. It is for this latter type of decision, and for developing the rules governing the former type, that the decision-making skills are required.

Decisions may be totally based on fact, they may be emotive or they may be a combination of the two. Decision making as a science really only concerns itself with fact. Operational research (such as critical path analysis), probability statistics and behavioural analysis are all different disciplines which can be utilised in this field to good effect, enabling the decision-maker to quantify factual knowledge, and hence reduce his reliance on subjective judgement, both at operational and organisational levels. The reader may be relieved to discover that it is not intended to expand upon these subjects at this juncture but, if he is particularly interested in factual decision making regarding maintenance problems, the books by A.K.S. Jardine on the subject are particularly to be recommended.

Purely emotive decisions are rare. One often hears of decisions being made by intuition, 'gut reaction' or 'the seat of the pants', but logic and fact often contribute significantly, since the subconscious, which influences such decisions, has been programmed by prior information and experience. In fact, the decision making process may be affected by many different aspects, such as:

(i) Psychology, philosophy and sociology on the emotive side.

(ii) Economics and efficiency, which are factual.

(iii) The environment, in the form of legislation, politics, etc., which may influence decisions in either an emotive or a factual way.

The decision-making skill, lies in the realisation and evaluation of these aspects.

113

5.4 *Training*

Technology is advancing at a great rate, thus maintenance training is becoming more and more important at a practical level, as maintainers need to be adequately trained to cope with increasingly complex equipment. While it is true to say that improved technology and design can reduce the degree of maintenance necessary on some items, training must still follow such improvements or the maintainer becomes out of touch with the equipment for which he is responsible. Also, more complex equipment often means more complex maintenance policies, thus heightening the importance of training at a maintenance management level.

We should, too, mention 'training-out' maintenance, i.e. training on the correct operation of equipment, thus cutting down equipment misuse and hence the amount of maintenance required. The importance of this type of training is also often raised by the increasing sophistication and complexity of equipment. It is not, however, when increased complexity of equipment is aimed towards automation, taking more and more control out of the hands of the operator.

If there is a weakness in maintenance training programmes, then it is usually in the lack of emphasis on the philosophies behind maintenance management. This is true not only in shipping but in industry generally. Education in these fundamental principles is vital, from as early in the training as possible. At higher levels, managers must be aware of these, as well as having the necessary management skills, in order to formulate successful maintenance policies. At all levels, personnel must be aware of the principles upon which their maintenance management system is based. In other words, they must know why they are being asked to do particular tasks. Not only that, but they must also be convinced that the reasoning behind the system is sound, and ultimately to their benefit. Only in this way can any degree of real commitment and motivation be expected. This training must be given to everybody involved – but always in a way that the recipient can understand – as soon as possible when a new scheme is being introduced to a fleet.

On a more general note, a look at some of the basic principles of training.

The main aims of training personnel are to increase their understanding, technical knowledge and skills, and to introduce them to new ideas and techniques. This benefits them personally by increasing their own potentials in their jobs. It benefits the organisation in which they work by providing adequate candidates for promotion, and hence helping to ensure the future of the company, and also by providing personnel who are more proficient, and efficient, in their jobs. Training, particularly that aimed at answering the 'why?' questions can, as mentioned above, also benefit both the organisation and the individual by providing commitment and motivation, as well as raising the level of morale and job satisfaction.

There are many different ways of effecting training. At 'practical' (rather than managerial) level, training consists of manufacturers' courses, Government and college courses and, at a more informal level, 'on the job' training and practical experience, plus manuals and possibly audio-visual devices, such as M.A.V.I.S., mentioned in the previous chapter. It should be emphasised here that training on maintenance of equipment is eased considerably if the equipment is standardised wherever possible.

At a managerial level, training consists of college courses, company 'in house' courses and seminars and consultants' courses. Informal training can be achieved by the distribution of company literature on management systems, etc. and, again, 'on the job' training, although it often requires a lot of personal enthusiasm and confidence on the part of a junior officer to question and become involved in a more senior officer's managerial functions – unless the management structure encourages it, such as including junior officers in management meetings etc.

Shipping companies should take advantage of all these methods of training, both in external organisations, such as colleges, and within their own organisation. Internal courses, seminars, etc. not only provide valuable training for personnel but are also an excellent opportunity for exchanging views

115

30

GENERAL SEAMANSHIP AND SAFETY (cont.)

Ref. No.	Task/Duty	Task/Duty Performed				Considered Satisfactory	
		Officer's Initials	Date	Officer's Initials	Date	Officer's Initials	Date
79	Assist with the " oiling round " of fairleads, tumblers, goose-necks etc.						
80	Sew and repair canvas						
81	Demonstrate use of safety harness and line (M544 & M605)						
82	Overhaul the patent log						
83	Assist with the inspection of cargo hooks, chains, swivels etc.						
84	Understand routine maintenance of: winches						
85	cranes						
86	capstans						
87	windlass						
88	Trim plug and cover ventilators						
89	Assist with the maintenance of: lifeboats						
90	lifeboat equipment and provisions						
91	launching davits and gear (M530)						
92	buoyant apparatus e.g. lifebuoys, lifejackets and attachments						

Give details of any tasks/duties which you have performed which are not listed in this Section

Make sure that you study all M Notices : M268, 320, 393, 439, 443, 447, 496, 498, 501, 527, 528, 530, 548, 570, 611, 651.

Fig. 43: Extract from MNTB Deck Cadet Record Book

31

CARGO WORK—GENERAL AND DRY CARGO SHIPS

Ref. No.	Task/Duty	Task/Duty Performed				Considered Satisfactory	
		Officer's Initials	Date	Officer's Initials	Date	Officer's Initials	Date
93	*Where applicable, assist in the opening & closing of hatches:* wood and canvas						
94	steel and single pull types						
95	hydraulic hatches						
96	deep tank lids						
97	insulated plugs						
98	handling and securing hatch beams						
99	Inspect and lubricate roller beams						
100	Assist with rigging clusters and portable lights						
101	Assist in general preparation of holds, including the laying of dunnage, for cargo						
102	Assist with separation of cargo						
103	*Assist in securing cargo:* stowed below deck						
104	stowed on deck						
105	Clean bilges, wells, and strum boxes (M467)						
106	Take ullages and temperatures, where applicable, of liquid cargo*						

Give details of any tasks/duties which you have performed which are not listed in this Section

*Any other associated tasks should be endorsed within the tanker cargo section.

and ideas between shore and sea staff. Company and manufacturers' literature, etc. can also be valuable as a training aid, but it must be prominently positioned, attractive to those for whom it is intended, and as easy as possible to digest. Private study on ships, as many readers will know, is not easy and companies should provide encouraging facilities, such as reading rooms, libraries and imaginitive training aids aboard ship.

One final but extremely important comment on training is that it should never be considered to be a 'one off' process. Training should be continuous, in one form or another, throughout a person's career, preventing stagnation and developing his or her potential to the full. In view of this it is only logical that a person's training should be planned, monitored and recorded, probably by his company's personnel department. This should not only include formal training on courses but also 'on the job' training and experience at different activities and tasks. A good example of how this might be achieved is the M.N.T.B.'s cadet record books, which show the studying, experience, etc. necessary through the apprenticeship, and are set out in such a way that this work is recorded as it is completed. Figure 43 shows an excerpt from such a book for a deck cadet. Quite a lot of the experience and 'on the job' training concerns maintenance, as can be seen from the excerpt. Similar record books for ratings are also available.

Ideally, plans and records should be drawn up, although perhaps not in such great detail as for a cadet, for all personnel throughout their career.

Chapter 6
Shipboard Management

6.1 *The Meaning*

Shipboard management is, essentially, the control loop within the ship. Referring back to the control of a ship, as shown in Figure 40, there are two loops, one between ship and shore and one within the ship. Generally, the stronger one loop becomes, the weaker the other. Thus, where the emphasis is upon shipboard management, the shore-to-ship control link may become looser.

The term 'Shipboard Management' is often used as if it is a new concept, but of course effective management of shipboard operations (maintenance being one of the larger operations, if not the largest) is, and always has been, essential on all ships, albeit to different degrees.

Certainly at present the trend is towards a greater degree of shipboard management, transferring more control and decision-making responsibility onto shipboard personnel. Sea staff can now possess management skills and tools, such as planning facilities and stock control systems, which were not available in those earlier days. By giving sea staff more management responsibility, along with the necessary training and facilities, it is possible to obtain the benefits of self-management, such as creating responsible ships' officers who are getting plenty of satisfaction out of their life at sea.

6.2 *Formal Policies*

Where shipboard management is a formally adopted policy by a company, or offered as a management system by a consultancy firm, this usually implies the setting up of a management team aboard each ship and supplying them with the necessary management tools. These tools, or facilities, could typically take the form of a work planning system (including a p.m. system), a recording and reporting system (reporting could be 'by exception' in this case since shore-to-ship control may be only occasional), and a stock control system (including catering stores and spares).

The management team could consist of:

The Master: ultimately responsible and chairman of the team.

The Chief Engineer: overall responsibility for maintenance aboard, particularly responsible for the p.m. and spares in engineering department.

The Chief Officer: responsible for p.m. and spares in deck department.

The 2nd Engineer and 2nd Deck Officer: assisting senior officers, advising on day to day work, etc., learning management procedures and skills.

The Catering Officer: responsible for catering and hotel cleaning, including catering and cleaning stores stock control.

The Radio Officer: responsible for radio and navigational electronic equipment maintenance and spares; overall supervision of system's paperwork.

The C.P.O.: responsible for deck and engineering spares store-keeping and day-to-day supervision of work by ratings.

The stated objectives of such formal systems presently in use appear to vary. Some aim simply to improve management aboard ship, by using a management team and management tools, and a more efficient but less cumbersome link with the shore, providing better feedback. Some set out with the clear aim of transferring responsibility to sea staff, thus cutting down drastically on the size and expense of their shore operation and, at the same time, creating more satisfied, committed, motivated and hence more efficient, sea staff.

There is little doubt now that some or all of these benefits are possible with such a system, provided it is well designed (bearing in mind the company and their operation), the sea staff are adequately trained and the policy is taken seriously.

6.3 *Traditional Policy*

The word 'traditional' here is simply intended to mean 'other than a formally adopted shipboard management policy'.

As has already been said, some degree of shipboard management is essential to the successful running of a ship, even when a company has not consciously adopted a formal policy. Therefore it is up to a ship's officers, under the leadership of the master, to formulate and put into practice the most effective management policy they are capable of. This does not necessarily mean they have to form themselves into complex planning boards or start keeping detailed records, but rather that they take stock of themselves, their crew, their ship, their management needs and management tools (e.g. p.m. system, spares stock control system, etc.), and then apply basic management principles – which often simply amounts to common sense. Regular (although not too frequent) meetings, at senior officer level and also possibly at lower levels down through the personnel structure, can help planning to become more effective, improve communications throughout the ship, and facilitate feedback information to senior officers (and hence ultimately, where necessary, to shore staff). Such meetings also encourage proper delegation, which should be an important feature of the policy. Delegation, provided the delegate is able to handle the duties given to him, can even out workloads, increase job satisfaction – by giving responsibility, and speed the 'learning by experience' process.

Thus everybody on board has the opportunity to not only know what is going on but also to have his say. He feels more involved, more committed, and hence does a better job.

6.4 *Shipboard Budgeting and Cost Awareness*

Shipboard budgeting can be taken to different degrees, depending on the amount and type of responsibility that the company wishes to give to the ship's officers in this area. It is often, though not always, a major part of a shipboard management system.

By budgeting, in this sense, we mean working within a total budget figure. Normally, this total is decided by head office rather than by the sea staff. However, there should be feedback from sea staff so that it can be adjusted as necessary. Costs, conditions and requirements are constantly changing, and if head office is prepared to trust sea staff to operate a budget they should be prepared to seriously consider their views on it.

Confining ourselves to the maintenance aspect, a shipboard budget may cover work done by shipboard personnel, by company shore personnel and by contracted shore labour; also materials (spares) and any shore facilities used.

With regard to the maintenance tasks, the budget may confine itself to cost associated with preventive and minor repair work or may include major work, such as extensive repairs or drydocking. If drydocking is not included in the shipboard budget, the budget should be linked to it in some way to prevent maintenance work included in the ship's budget being cut back at the expense of the drydocking budget.

Shore labour costs, if they are to be included in the shipboard budget, are relatively easy to obtain, but the ship's crew labour costs, if these also are to be included, are more nebulous. Are all ranks to be included in the costing? Is just overtime to be considered or all working hours? These are but two questions which spring to mind.

With regard to the cost of materials, the cost of stock (perhaps only special items, outside normal expected usage, but preferably all stock) being *ordered* during the budget period should be considered. To consider the cost of stock being *used* during the period is not so realistic since the cost at purchase may not be the same as at the time of use.

By considering the items which it is possible to include under a shipboard budget it can be seen that the budget is very closely linked with the authority, or responsibility, given to the officers in the management team for the operation and maintenance of their ship. If they are to successfully carry this responsibility they must know precisely what is, and what is not, included in their budget, i.e. the extent of their authority.

For shipboard budgeting to work, there are three important requisites.

Firstly, the budget must be *realistic*. It must be big enough to cover the ship's needs and sufficiently flexible, allowing adequate freedom for the shipboard managers to plan. The budget period must also be realistic. This will vary with ship type, operation and so on, but generally nothing less than a year would be acceptable. Ideally the same shipboard managers should stay with the ship for the whole budget period, so that they can follow their budget plan through. The fact that this is not practicable for many types of company operations is, perhaps, one of the main reasons why shipboard budgeting is not widely adopted.

Secondly, those officers on the ship who are to administer the budget must be *adequately trained* to do so, and must appreciate its significance and the different ways in which its use can be optimised.

The third requisite is closely related to the second. It is that *sufficient information* must be available aboard the ship to enable the officers to administer the budget. This information, relating primarily though not exclusively to cost, must consist of historical data (obtainable from records analysis), and data concerning the present (current prices, etc) and the future (expected trends, shortages, etc). Apart from the records kept on board, it is up to the shore operation to supply the ship with this information.

Where shipboard budgeting is adopted, the ship's personnel will almost certainly become more cost conscious, since they are now directly concerned. This is obviously good for the shipping company, but it is also good for the personnel since they can, by cutting costs in some areas, spend more of their budget in other more preferable ones.

A cost awareness policy by the company, such as regularly informing the ship of spares costs (perhaps by showing the costs on the packing notes arriving with the spares) is a worthwhile exercise, even if budgeting is not achieved. Provided the ship's crew absorb this information, by recording it and propagating it, they can appreciate the value of specific items and thus will be encouraged to use and re-order them in a reasonable way. A cost awareness policy also acts as a good 'lead-in' to a shipboard budgeting policy, getting shipboard personnel used to costs, before transferring the onus of budgeting onto them.

6.5 *General Requirements*

Taking a broad view of shipboard management, including budgeting, it is possible to see several general requirements.

The overall policy must be realistic, bearing in mind existing limitations, such as:

(i) The type of ship and her run.

(ii) The background and training of shipboard personnel.

(iii) The time available to shipboard personnel during the voyage.

(iv) The facilities from the company ashore, within the ship and in foreign ports.

The officers must be trained in the necessary management skills and in the use of the necessary management tools.

The crew, or at least the officers involved in the management, must stay with the ship for adequate time spans. As previously mentioned in relation to shipboard budgeting, they must be able to follow through their own plan and their decisions. This is often a serious problem. If it is not possible for men to stay on one ship for this long a time, one alternative solution is to have a crew rotation system, where a man returns to the same ship after his leave. For this to work, however, *all* those participating in the management for the period considered must be involved in the planning at the start of the period.

Finally, there must be adequate back-up facilities for the type of management system adopted, mainly in the way of management tools – such as reporting and recording systems, a stock control system and a p.m. system. Coupled to this is the need for sufficient information to be received aboard to ensure effective management. It is not suggested, however, that all these things are necessary in a sophisticated form. If

124

the shipboard management is to be of a simple form, then so should the back-up facilities.

To conclude this chapter, we should perhaps spare some thoughts for the shore staff. As stated earlier, one of the aims of shipboard maintenance is a reduction in the size of the shore operation. So, if the shipboard personnel are to gain responsibility, the shore personnel must be prepared to lose it. In the extreme, this could mean that the shore staff who remain (since their numbers may be reduced) will act far more as a service to the ships, when required, than as a control over them.

Chapter 7
Requirements of
Regulatory Bodies

7.1 *General Comments*

The majority of rules and regulations, statutory or otherwise, are concerned with safety. They may concern safety of the maintainers, of the operators, of the users or anybody else who may be involved – quite possibly the general public when considering, say, pollution or explosion risks. It is therefore the responsibility of the maintainer to ensure the availability, efficiency and hence safety of the items being considered. This responsibility is enforced by the regulations which lay down standards and, to ensure that these standards are met, impose periodic surveys.

This chapter will not be too specific in its description of the regulations (which would require a further book) but will simply outline the intentions of the different acts, rules, regulations and recommendations, and the areas which they cover.

7.2 *Health and Safety at Work Act*

The Health and Safety at Work Act of 1974 is designed primarily to replace the Factories Acts. In essence, it gives the relevant Ministers the powers necessary to introduce their own regulations to replace the Factories Acts, but as yet few specific regulations pertinent to our area of interest have been introduced. Most of the relevant sections of the Factories Acts, therefore, still stand (including the Dock Regulations empowered by the Factories Act).

The Factories Act of 1961 was designed primarily to safeguard employees' welfare, safety and health. The Act specifies periodic overhauls, cleaning, surveys, etc. of many items

126

of equipment, considering the safety and well-being of the operators, associated personnel and also the maintainers of the equipment. As well as requiring examinations, inspections, etc. of certain items at stated intervals, the Act requires the keeping of reports of these examinations for future reference, and that equipment shall bear a distinguishing mark. It also makes preventive maintenance of some items obligatory.

The main surveys arising from these Acts are those relating to lifting gear, carried out by a qualified inspector at the time of installation and after repairs, and periodically by the chief officer or some other competent person. Certain cables, blocks, shackles, etc. also require annealing and inspection at specified intervals.

7.3 *Merchant Shipping Acts and Regulations*

The Merchant Shipping Act of 1979 put into effect the 1974 International Convention for the Safety of Life at Sea. This 1979 Act, together with earlier Merchant Shipping Acts, gave power to subsequent Statutory Instruments, such as the following:

Passenger Ship Construction Regulations 1980 (S.I. 535);
Cargo Ship Construction and Survey Regulations 1980 (S.I. 537);

These rules lay down constructional and safety standards and give details of surveys to be carried out prior to the issue of the various safety certificates as well as some intermediate surveys (with the exception of passenger ship construction surveys which are specified in the 1894 and 1964 M.S. Acts). The main surveys are:

Annual surveys for the issue of Passenger and Safety Certificate of passenger ships, covering construction, safety equipment, radio equipment, subdivision load lines etc;
Annual surveys for the issue of Safety Radiotelegraphy or Safety Radiotelephony Certificates of cargo ships;
Biennial surveys for the issue of Safety Equipment Certificate for cargo ships;

Regulatory Bodies

Surveys for the issue of Cargo Ship Safety Construction Certificate, valid for five years.

Intermediate surveys for the retention of the above certificate are as follows:

Hull and ship side fastenings (plus fire resistive divisions, doors, ventilation ducts and baffles for tankers and combination carriers) *every two and a half years*;
Ship side fittings every five years;
Watertube boilers and steam generators internally and externally every two years, and annually if over eight years old;
Pressure vessels (e.g. starting air bottles);
Propeller shafts, if oil lubricated or with continuous liners usually to be withdrawn every five years, other shafts every two years.

The Merchant Shipping (Load Lines) Act of 1967 put the International Convention on Load Lines 1966 into effect, requiring merchant ships to have a suitable Load Line Certificate and giving power to the Load Line Rules 1968 (S.I. 1053). These Rules cover:

Strength (requirements of Assigning Authority);
Watertight and weathertight integrity of all openings overside and in deck (hatches, discharges, etc) *and their efficient working* (a maintenance requirement);
Protection of the crew, e.g. guard rails, gangways etc.

The Rules require a major survey in relation to the above to be carried out when the vessel is new, for the assignment of the Load Line and the issue of the Load Line Certificate (which is valid for five years), and prior to the issue of each new certificate. Intermediate, approximately annual, surveys must also be carried out to ensure that fittings and appliances for the protection of openings, guard rails, freeing ports and means of access to crew's quarters are in effective condition, and that no changes to the ship have taken place that would render inaccurate the data on which freeboard was assigned.

The M.S. Act 1970 states that the DoT may make regulations requiring the maintenance, inspection and testing of

128

any equipment. The M.S. Act 1979, in its discussion of safety and health on ships, says that the Secretary of State may make regulations on maintenance, repair, inspection and surveying of ships and their machinery and equipment. Statutory Instruments, including such regulations, are at present being drawn up and will be empowered by these two Acts.

7.4   *Dock Work Convention*

In June 1979, an International Labour Conference adopted the 'Convention and Recommendation concerning occupational safety and health in dock work'. The Health & Safety Commission (who have published the document) have advised early ratification of this convention, probably during 1980. It is, however, open to question how much of the convention is to be included in regulations and how much in supporting codes and guidance notes. It is also open to discussion what form the regulations should take (e.g. empowered by which Act) and who should issue the codes and guidance notes. It should also be noted that some of the provisions of the Convention are already satisfied by the existing Health and Safety at Work Act, 1974, the Factories Act, 1961 and the Dock Regulations, 1934.

The reason for considering this convention here is that, in its concern for occupational safety and health in dock work, it very much concerns the maintenance, testing, examination and inspection of cargo gear, cargo safety equipment and all cargo work-places, i.e. down hatches, on deck, etc. The convention states that all cargo gear (i.e. lifting appliances and loose gear), including slings and grabs as well as the larger items such as cranes, should be maintained in 'good repair and working order'. They should also, it says, be tested in accordance with national laws or regulations by a competent person (i.e. a person possessing the necessary knowledge and experience and acceptable as such to the competent authority) before being put into use for the first time or after any substantial alteration or repair affecting its safety.

Ship's lifting appliances should be retested at least every five years. The tests should be followed by a thorough examination. In addition, all gear should be examined and certified by a competent person every twelve months. Thorough examination is taken to mean a visual examination supplemented by any other means if necessary in order to reliably conclude that the item is safe. All loose gear should be regularly inspected before use by a responsible person (i.e. a person appointed by the employer, the master or the owner of the gear who has sufficient knowledge, experience and the requisite authority).

The convention also requires authenticated records to be kept (on shore or on board) providing evidence of the safe condition of all lifting appliances and loose gear, showing S.W.L.s and the dates and results of all tests, examinations and inspections (except the regular inspection before use, in which case a record need only be made if a defect is discovered). A register of all cargo gear should also be kept, comprising all certificates granted or recognised as valid (or certified copies) in respect of all testing, examination and inspection.

The convention states that gear should not be used if either the certification or the gear itself is found to be unsatisfactory by the competent authority (authorised by the Member country).

In short the convention is laying down a p.m. system for all cargo gear. It requires a register and records to be kept and the condition of the gear to be continually monitored, as well as being subjected to periodical examination. The maintenance policy is preventive, the ultimate consideration being safety. Ideally, this p.m. policy for cargo gear should be incorporated into the overall p.m. system for the ship.

7.5 *Classification Society Rules and Surveys* (Lloyd's Register)

Classification societies make extensive rules on the construction and efficiency of operation of ships, their machinery and their equipment. These rules are not statutory requirements in themselves but, unless a vessel is classed, i.e. has complied with the relevant rules, her owners will find it very difficult to obtain Load Line and Safety Construction Certificates, insurance, cargo contracts, etc. To stay in class, a ship is subject to certain surveys specified by the classification society.

Annual surveys, which are combined with statutory and other load line surveys where practicable, are required and cover such items as steering arrangements, vent piping and fire appliances.

Drydock surveys are required every two to two and a half years, for inspection of the shell, openings to the sea, the rudder, the propeller, etc. In-water surveys for ships less than ten years old, other than passenger vessels, are permitted in lieu of docking surveys, provided that the diving and survey operations are carried out by firms recognised by the classification society and that a drydock will follow if further survey and repair work is found necessary. (The firms carrying out these in-water surveys claim considerable economic saving for the shipowner).

Special surveys are required on the hull, the severity of these increasing with the ship's age. Some inspection items under these surveys (such as the lifting of the rudder for inspection of the pintles) necessitate drydocking. These surveys become due at four yearly intervals.

Complete surveys of machinery are also required every four years.

The ship owner can, however, opt for the *Continuous Survey* scheme (both for the hull and the machinery, or either). Regarding the hull, all compartments must be opened for survey and tested in rotation, with an interval of five years between consecutive examinations of each part. Regarding machinery, the various items (possibly one to two hundred items selected when the ship was new) are opened for survey in rotation to ensure that, as far as practicable, the interval between consecutive examinations of each item does not exceed five years, and that about one fifth of the surveys are completed annually.

There is also a scheme where the chief engineer, provided that he holds a first class certificate of competency and has been employed by the owners for at least three years whilst holding this certificate, may survey and overhaul some parts

131

of machinery, on behalf of the classification society, while the ship is at sea or in a port where the society is not represented. Confirmatory surveys on items surveyed by a chief engineer are carried out by a classification society surveyor at the earliest convenience, but this latter type of survey is mainly in the nature of an operational test, to confirm the thoroughness of the chief engineer's survey. To give some examples, the chief engineer may survey such items as: main engine cylinder covers; valves; cylinder liners; pistons and rods; main engine and independently driven pumps; air compressors; windlass.

7.6 *Recommendations*

Apart from regulations concerning maintenance, there are also recommendations, of varied severity, coming from several different sources.

Firstly, there are 'M' Notices from the Department of Trade. These are basically recommendations of good practice. Like many recommendations from authoritative bodies, in practice one must take heed of them or else risk accusations of negligence, having an unseaworthy vessel and so on. 'M' Notices usually concern safety, and therefore those relating to maintenance may generally be divided into two groups: Notices involving the proper and frequent maintenance of safety equipment (e.g. M. 866 on Maintenance of Liferaft Disengaging Gears, or M. 765 on Maintenance of Fire Appliances), or those involving maintenance procedures regarding safety of maintainers, operators etc (e.g. M. 752, Electric Shock Hazard in the Use of Electric Arc Welding Plant).

Secondly, and also from the DoT, there is the Code of Safe Working Practices for Merchant Seamen. This publication covers, in some depth, safe practices to be adhered to while carrying out various maintenance tasks, maintenance work relating to the safety of a ship and her equipment (e.g. it warns against painting over cracked or rotten timber on stairways, etc.), and maintenance of safety equipment. This code includes points raised in 'M' Notices, presenting them in a co-ordinated and often in a somewhat simpler form.

Thirdly, IMCO (Inter-Governmental Maritime Consultative Organisation) make a vast number of recommendations across the whole spectrum of shipboard operations, many relating to maintenance – perhaps by setting performance specifications, by recommending survey or test frequencies or by describing maintenance procedures. Like 'M' Notices, IMCO recommendations are not in themselves strictly legal requirements but, in time, many of them are accepted (with or without modification) by this and other countries as statutory requirements.

Fourthly, we have the recommendations of the General Council of British Shipping, supported by the shipping companies. Most of these recommendations concern operational rather than maintenance activities on board (e.g. Tanker Safety Guide), but they may make indirect or implied recommendations, such as equipment being up to certain standards of efficiency, etc.

Next, there are the various institutes, such as the Nautical Institute, the Institution of Electrical Engineers or the Institute of Marine Engineers. All these institutes make recommendations and give advice to their respective professions, drawing on the experience of their members and experts in the various fields. Some of these recommendations become legal requirements if they are accepted by the Department of Trade, such as the Institution of Electrical Engineers' Regulations for the Electrical and Electronic Equipment of Ships, empowered by the Cargo Ship Construction and Survey Rules.

Lastly, seafarers' training bodies, such as the M.N.T.B. (Merchant Navy Training Board) and the A.N.S. (Association of Navigation Schools), make recommendations to the Department of Trade, the colleges and the shipping companies. These recommendations may concern formal training in the classroom, less formal training such as correspondence courses, reading or audio visual aids, or 'on the job' training and experience – the last of these being more the province of the M.N.T.B. Since a fairly large part of shipboard operations concerns maintenance activities, many of these recommendations relate to maintenance (see the earlier example of the M.N.T.B. Deck Cadet Record Book).

7.7   Surveys

All the surveys, mentioned in the previous sections of this chapter, could perhaps be looked upon as 'enforced condition monitoring'. The Government, the classification societies and the various advisory bodies all specify the surveys they think are necessary in order to monitor adequately the condition of the parts of the ship and her equipment with which they are concerned. Should a survey reveal a condition inferior to a predetermined standard, the situation must be rectified.

Where possible, classification surveys, load line surveys, safety construction surveys, etc. are combined to reduce the costs involved (out of service or downtime costs, drydock costs, etc). The classification society surveyors can usually also cover the statutory surveys thus, for example, an annual classification survey and an annual load line survey can, in effect, become one survey by one surveyor.

All surveys, those specified by the various bodies and those which must be devised to ensure the standards required by the bodies, should be incorporated into the overall long-term maintenance master plan, and subsequent short-term planning.

Chapter 8
Conclusions for the Future

8.1 *Development*

Up until recent times, the master and officers of a merchant ship were left to manage most of the shipboard operations. Certainly they almost totally managed shipboard maintenance with little or no control, guidance or training from their owners. Realisation, by the more enlightened in the shipping industry, of the importance of effective maintenance management coincided with the beginning of the 'computer age' and the related trend towards centralisation. This, perhaps, explains why most of the initial p.m. schemes tended to place control more with head office than with the ship. After a time, however, the disadvantages of this type of scheme became apparent (excessive rigidity of planning, extensive paperwork, under-use and lack of commitment of sea staff), and the trend reverted to shipboard management, which appeared to overcome these disadvantages. So, you might say, have we come full circle? In a sense perhaps yes, but we have learnt a lot on the way about shipboard maintenance management, about the communications involved and about the necessary training of sea staff.

With the advent of the silicon chip and micro-electronics, mini-computers on board ship are becoming common place. Such computers could well be used for storing and displaying maintenance related data (the display could perhaps be of the T.V. type). This could easily provide back-up information, out-dating manuals and even microfilm. These computers might also be used to assist in the planning of maintenance, the displaying of the plan, recording and analysis. They would, in all likelihood, also considerably reduce the need for extensive computer facilities in head office, being able to store, cross-reference and retrieve spares ordering information, for example.

Preventive maintenance based on monitoring, rather than on scheduling, is also seen by many to be more economical, more effective and ultimately more desirable where it is feasible. This approach often requires on-the-spot judgement and planning.

It would therefore appear that both the growth of micro-technology and the feeling of desirability for monitoring-based maintenance support the trend towards increasing the responsibility of ships' staff for maintenance management.

8.2 Probable Future Needs

Whichever way technology takes us, the basic maintenance philosophies – i.e. the various policies open to us, the planned maintenance system components, etc. – are unlikely to change. The forms which they take, however, undoubtedly will, as briefly discussed in the previous section. As the world's resources, such as steel and oil, get more and more expensive, so the need for maintenance rather than replacement will grow in the shipping industry as in other industries. Thus the future will see ship operators constantly looking for improved maintenance methods and management.

Automation in ships is already upon us, unmanned machinery space (U.M.S.) vessels being commonplace, and this is creating new maintenance needs as well as new maintenance opportunities.

On U.M.S. ships, where alarm systems are extensively used (involving sensors and electronic circuitry), preventive maintenance, while being desirable in the interests of safety and major machinery repair costs, is often difficult to achieve since the components of these systems often have random life spans. Also, the monitoring sensors are by no means perfected, often being adversely affected by vibration and heat. However, various testing procedures are normally incorporated into a programme which is on-going throughout a ship's life. This programme is sometimes separate from, and sometimes included in, a vessel's p.m. system, though the latter is preferable for planning, recording, and subsequent analysis. It should, perhaps, be noted here that the various classification societies seem to differ widely on the extent of the alarm system testing programme. Some are over-extensive (unintentionally tempting the engineer to short-cut them) while others are somewhat scanty.

Maintenance management is facilitated by automation, since personnel are free to spend more time on maintenance. On the other hand, since one of the main reasons for automation is the ability to reduce manning levels, and automation generally means more complex equipment, there is a particular need for the maintenance management to be as effective as possible.

At the present time, shipping companies operating p.m. systems aboard their ships appear to make no distinction between the types of system for automated and standard vessels. Usually, these are scheduled preventive maintenance systems, although there is some use of portable condition monitoring equipment mainly for auxiliary equipment. As mentioned earlier, monitoring-based maintenance (condition and performance monitoring) is likely to expand, although the forms it will take are not yet clear. So far as the author can ascertain, monitoring equipment incorporated in automated vessels (alarm systems, data loggers, etc) is not used for monitoring-based maintenance, at least the use of such equipment is not included in any formalised shipboard maintenance management systems. It appears that the main reasons are that this monitoring equipment has not so far been designed with monitoring-based maintenance in mind, and also that the sensors involved are not sufficiently reliable or suitable for this type of application. It does, however, seem logical that with design advancement and improved sensors, monitoring systems will ultimately have a dual role; firstly, to enable equipment to become automated and, secondly, to allow maintenance of much of this equipment to be based on monitoring rather than scheduling. In this way, automation could not only aid shipboard management by permitting more

137

time to be spent on maintenance, but also provide a facility which could allow maintenance management aboard ship to be more effective.

8.3 *Training Needs*

There is a need for training of seagoing personnel in maintenance management and its attendant philosophies as well as practical maintenance.

It is very important that sea staff should understand the philosophies behind their company's p.m. system, and be aware of the advantages both to their company and to them individually. An increase in managerial capability (in senior ranks), and commitment and job satisfaction (in all ranks) should follow.

'On the job' training is in most cases sadly lacking, at both management and practical levels. At a management level, second and third engineers and second mates could greatly benefit by occasional inclusion in the management team; e.g. on ships where planning meetings are held, these officers should occasionally sit in on these meetings, perhaps on a rota basis.

The system of initial training of sea staff, relating to various companies' p.m. and spares systems, which seems to be most prevalent is as follows.

When a system is installed on board a vessel the personnel to sail on that vessel are given some training, mainly concerning the operation of the system, although in some cases an effort is made to explain the philosophy behind the system. This training may be carried out on board the ship, prior to the voyage or (for the management team) on shore courses lasting several days. The disadvantage of this system is that the personnel on board that ship will, after a comparatively short period, probably be replaced by others, who may not have had the benefit of this training and must simply be guided by a manual on the systems operation which, hopefully, would be left aboard the vessel. It is therefore very important that sea staff throughout the fleet, or at least those who might find themselves responsible for the management of the system, be formally trained as swiftly as possible, prior to and during the installation of the system throughout the fleet.

The question now arises as to who should be responsible for this training. The ideal solution, not yet achieved in full, is for the merchant navy officer to receive training in all the basic maintenance management principles involved, along with his standard training, while at college. It would then be up to the shipping company or consultancy firm to acquaint him with the system with which he is to work, which he would then find relatively easy to understand and accept.

Training at a practical level must constantly be changing, keeping up with the development of new equipment and techniques – such as various forms of condition monitoring, automated equipment, handling equipment for new types of cargo and new hull and tank protective coatings. Much of this sort of training is best achieved 'on the job', and encouragement should be given to those involved by others on board and also by the company, by providing the necessary training aids aboard and sending the personnel on manufacturers' courses.

As mentioned earlier in the book, sea staff are, to a fairly large extent, both the operators and maintainers of the vessel's equipment. Their training is therefore designed with this in mind. However, with the advent of more and more sophisticated and automated equipment, coupled with the reduction in manning levels, one must wonder how this situation will change. Will operators become separate from maintainers? Who will manage maintenance? Will the amount of maintenance on board ship reduce? These questions cannot yet be answered with certainty, but it is clear that the training needs of the future depend on their answers, and that the training of seafarers must keep abreast of these needs.

8.4   Final Comments

Effective shipboard maintenance management relies on the same principles as any form of management; sound planning, good communications and last but certainly not least the application of logic and common sense. By good communications we should include, not only efficient paperwork but, perhaps more importantly, good working relationships between all those involved, aboard ship and ashore.

Where p.m. and spares systems are installed aboard ship, they should be looked upon, and used, by sea staff as *tools* to assist them in achieving the standards of maintenance required, advantageous to both them and their company. They should not be seen as a hindrance but as a help, and if seen as the former, either the attitude of the sea staff is wrong (perhaps due to a lack of training) or the systems are wrong, or both. In any event, it is up to the company to put this right, considering carefully the views of the sea staff.

If a company has not installed formal maintenance management systems aboard their ships, as a conscious policy decision or otherwise, the responsible officers should endeavour to formulate systems to suit their needs, but these systems should be kept as simple as possible. A notebook in a boiler suit pocket can sometimes be as good as or better than several planning boards!

Finally, whatever form maintenance management on board ship takes, it must be dynamic. Schedules that are too rigid and records that are never used are worse than useless; they are actively harmful. Like those who seek to practise it, maintenance management should be adaptable and constantly seeking improvement.

Bibliography

1. *Communications within Planned Maintenance Systems at Sea.* B.E.M. Thomas, (Liverpool Polytechnic Publication).
2. *Principles of Planned Maintenance.* R.H. Clifton.
3. *Optimising Ship Repair and Maintenance Costs; A Systematic Approach.* J.B. Bunnis, (N.E. Coast Institute of Shipbuilders and Engineers (Nov. '73)).
4. *Ship Maintenance: A Quantitive Approach.* Shields, Sparshott & Cameron.
5. *A New Approach to Ship Maintenance.* B.K. Batten, (Institute of Marine Engineers (Jan. '76)).
6. *Maintenance Management with Particular Regard to Automatic Equipment on Ships.* B.E.M. Thomas, (Safety at Sea, 4th International Symposium 1978).
7. *Decision Making in Maintenance.* A.K.S. Jardine, (Institute of Mechanical Engineers ('74)).
8. *Operational Research in Maintenance.* A.K.S. Jardine.
9. *Effective Maintenance Management.* E.T. Newbrough.
10. *Management Information and Systems.* A.G. Donald.
11. *Information Theory.* J.F. Young.

Index

Analysis of, p.m. records, 24, 36
  spares records, 43
Audio-visual systems, 87, 88
Automation, 136
Availability of equipment, 20

Breakdown, definition, 7
  maintenance, 7
  policy, 6
  replacements, 6
Budget, control, 24
  shipboard budgeting, 121

Calendar time scheduling, 8
Check lists, 88
Classification Society rules, 130
Codes, 25, 42, 52, 66, 94, 108, 109
Comments, final, 139
Communications, 102
Computers, 37, 47, 135
Condition, analysis, 10
  monitoring, 10
Construction regulations, 127
Consultants, 49, 62
Continuous survey, 131
Continuity, 23
Control systems, 99, 119
Control, types, 100
  sources, 101
Costs of, ship and equipment, 12
  shore labour, 13
  spares, 13
  shipboard cost awareness, 121
  high cost areas, 24
Coverage of equipment, 21

Decision making, 110
Deterioration of equipment, 3

Development, 135
Diagrams, operational sequence, 66
  unit location, 88
Downtime, 3
  cost of, 13

Efficiency, of equipment, 3, 20

Forecasting, 24
Future needs, 136

General Council of British
  Shipping, 133

Health and Safety at Work Act, 126
Human facors, 106

IMCO Recommendations, 133
Information, back-up, 86
  collection, 104
  transmission & reception, 104
Information theory, 107
Inventory, for p.m., 25
  for spares, 40
Isolation, degree of, 12
Issue, of spares, 44, 48
In-water surveys, 131

Job specifications (Job cards), 30,
  66, 71

Labour, effective use of, 21
Load Line Rules, 128

Maintenance, definition, 4
  factors, 11
  objectives, 2

Maintenance (*cont.*)
 policies, 4, 15
 problems, 2
Manuals, operating and
  maintenance, 62, 86, 87
 manufacturers, 80
 spares, 41, 94
Manufacturer, p.m. & spares
  example, 71
Merchant Shipping Acts &
  Regulations, 127
Microfiche, 87, 98
'M' Notices, 132
Monitoring, 10, 136, 137
Morale, 23

Operational research, 16, 17
Options of systems, 49
Ordering spares, 44, 59, 81
 automatic spares ordering, 47

Performance monitoring, 10, 11
Planned maintenance, benefits, 20
 components, 25
 definition, 18
 meaning, 18
 system examples, 51, 62, 71, 83
Plans, Master Plan (long-term), 31,
  52
 Planning Facility (short-term),
  68, 69
Policy statement, p.m., 27
 spares, 41
Preventive maintenance, 7, 8
 policy, 6
 replacement, 6

Recommendations, 132
Records, general, 19
 p.m., 36, 52, 74, 84
 spares, 43, 57
Receipts of spares, 44, 47
Register of equipment, 25
Regulations, 126
Replacement policy, 5

Repairs, emergency, 21
Reporting, by exception, 35, 66,
  107, 120
 maintenance work, 35, 54, 74, 83
 spares, 44, 59
Running maintenance, 8
Running time scheduling, 9

Safe Working Practices, Code of,
  132
Scheduling, 8, 74
Shipboard management, general
  requirements, 124
 policies, formal, 119
  traditional, 121
 meaning of, 119
 training, 63
Shut-down maintenance, 8
Spares control, components, 39
 importance, 38
 objectives, 38
 order/receipt/issue
  documentation, 44
 planning, 23
 policy, 41
 records, 43
 system examples, 54, 81, 97
Stocktaking, 48
Storage of spares, 47
Storekeeping, 47
Surveys, classification society, 129
 general, 28, 132
 load line, 128
 safety, 127

Time for tasks, 28, 29
Training, general, 114, 138
 bodies, 133

U.M.S. ships, 136
Uniformity of ships, 14

Vibration analysis, 10, 62

Weaknesses, highlighted by p.m.,
  24
Work study, 28